Choosing Your RV
HOME BASE

SECOND EDITION

Published by:

Roundabout Publications
PO Box 19235
Lenexa, KS 66285

800-455-2207

www.TravelBooksUSA.com

Published by Roundabout Publications, PO Box 19235, Lenexa, KS 66285 / 800-455-2207

Library of Congress Control Number: 2010924947

ISBN-10: 1-885464-33-9
ISBN-13: 978-1-885464-33-0

Contents

Introduction

The full-time RV lifestyle comes with many wonderful benefits, including the freedom to travel anywhere in this great country. That freedom, however, doesn't include escaping the realities of paying taxes and other legal matters such as registering a vehicle or obtaining a driver's license. Without proper planning, these common issues can become a challenge for the full-time RVer.

While it's possible to have a driver's license from one state, your vehicle registered in another state, and "live" somewhere else, this practice is not advised. Without a clearly established home base or domicile, it is possible that you could become liable for taxes in more than one state.

To avoid any potential complications, your best option is to establish a home base. This should be the state where your vehicle is registered, where you obtain your driver's license, register to vote, have your bank account, acquire your insurance and all the other necessities of life. This will also be the state in which you pay your taxes.

Choosing a home base can be an important decision. There are many factors that must be considered. Simply selecting a state that has the lowest (or no) state income tax is not always your best option. For example, a state with high income taxes may have a lower sales tax rate or vehicle registration fee. Some states rely heavily on property taxes for their revenue so they may have a lower income tax rate. This book provides a wealth of information to help you narrow your home base search.

It is recommended you use this book in combination with further research tailored to your specific needs. This can be a time-consuming process but the savings can be significant.

The full-time RV lifestyle gives you the unique opportunity to choose any state to call "home." It is important to remember that your home base decision need not be permanent. As your personal situation changes, so can your home base if it's to your advantage.

How to Use This Book

The following is an explanation of the information included for each state. Due to the nature of this information (taxes, fees, regulations, etc.) the rules can and do change. Before reaching any final decision, it is best to confirm the information provided.

WEATHER

	Huntsville			Mobile		
	🌡	💧	❄	🌡	💧	❄
Jan	49/31	5	1.5	61/39	5	0.1
Feb	55/34	5	0.7	65/42	5.2	0.2
Mar	63/41	6.6	0.4	71/49	6.6	0.1
Apr	72/48	4.8	0	77/55	5.3	0
May	80/57	5.1	0	84/63	5.6	0
Jun	87/65	4.3	0	89/69	5.3	0
Jul	89/70	4.6	0	91/72	7.7	0
Aug	89/68	3.5	0	91/72	6.8	0
Sep	83/62	4.1	0	87/68	6	0
Oct	73/50	3.3	0	79/56	3	0
Nov	62/41	4.7	0	70/48	4.2	0
Dec	52/34	5.7	0.2	63/42	5.4	0.1

🌡	Average monthly high and low temperatures in degrees Fahrenheit.
💧	Average monthly precipitation totals in inches.
❄	Average monthly snowfall totals in inches.

WEATHER

It's always nice to know the weather conditions in advance. In this case, historical averages will have to do! You might find the variances, even within the same state, interesting.

STATE AND LOCAL TAXES

State Sales Tax (%) 4.00
Exempt: prescription drugs.
Local Sales Taxes (up to an additional %) 8.00
Inheritance Tax ....No
Estate Tax.. Yes
Limited to federal estate tax collection

STATE AND LOCAL TAXES

State Sales Tax

Only four states do not collect sales tax (AK, MT, NH, and OR). Four additional states (AZ, DE, HI, and NM) have a Gross Receipts Tax in lieu of a sales tax. A gross receipts tax is imposed on the business instead of the customer. The rate usually varies depending on the business activity. The tax is usually passed on to the customer in the form of a higher price. Most businesses will show an amount on your receipt that they added to cover their cost of the tax.

A few states have a single statewide rate but most allow local governments to add to the base tax rate. The state sales tax can range from a low of 2.9% (CO) to a high of 8.25% (CA).

Local Sales Taxes

In Alabama, the highest, local rates can add up to an additional 8%. Hawaii comes in with the lowest rate at 1/2%. Arkansas wins the top spot with a combined state and local tax rate of 12.5%. Fourteen states including the District of Columbia have no local sales tax.

Inheritance Tax

At the current time, 10 states have some form of an inheritance tax. If this is a factor for you, check with the state for specifics; rules and limits vary with each state.

Estate tax

At present, 39 states (includes the District of Columbia) have some form of an estate tax. If this is a factor for you, check with the state for specifics; rules and limits vary with each state.

PERSONAL INCOME TAXES

State Income Tax (%) .... 3.5 - 6.45
  3 income brackets - Lowest $15,000; Highest $30,000.

Personal Exemption $ (single / joint) ...... 2,250 / 4,500
Standard Deduction $ (single / joint)...... 3,000 / 6,000
  Additional $850 if age 65 or over.

Federal Income Tax Paid - Deduction Allowed ..... None
Social Security Income - Tax Exempt .... Limits
  Exempt if federal adjusted gross income is $75,000 or less.

Retired Military Pay - Tax Exempt .... Yes
State & Local Government Pensions - Tax Exempt .... Limits
  Full exemption for Kansas state pensions, none for out-of-state pensions.

Federal Civil Service Pensions - Tax Exempt .... Yes
Railroad Retirement - Tax Exempt .... Yes
Private Pension - Tax Exempt .... No

PERSONAL INCOME TAXES

State Income Tax

Most states impose an income tax. Alaska, Florida, Nevada, South Dakota, Texas, Washington, and Wyoming don't have an income tax. Tennessee and New Hampshire tax only interest and dividend income. Seven states (CO, IL, IN, MA, MI, PA, and UT) have a flat tax rate, others use a graduated scale based on income. In addition, county or city level income taxes may be imposed in 14 states.

Tax rates are shown along with the number and range of the income brackets. The tax brackets are for single taxpayers or married people filing separate returns. Some states will increase or double the bracket widths for joint filers to avoid a marriage penalty.

Personal Exemption and Standard Deduction

Shown are the deduction amounts for both "single filers" and "married, filing a joint return."

Federal Income Tax Paid

This indicates which states allow a deduction for any taxes paid on your federal return.

Retirement Income

The rest of this section covers six types of pension and retirement income and the tax exempt status for each. A "Yes," "No," or "Limits" answer is provided for each retirement income type.

A general explanation for "Limits" is found either below the pension type or at the end with a common note that relates to all. Limits are usually based on age, income, or a maximum amount that can be deducted.

Rules vary by state and type of pension (and there are exceptions to the rules). Be sure to get all the specific details for your type of retirement income before reaching any conclusions.

VEHICLES

Registration Fees .... 2 Years
   Passenger vehicles, $77. The very first registration period is four years (double the rate), every two years thereafter.

   Camper and travel trailer, $81. Add $6.75 for each additional foot over 10 feet. (No vehicle over 45 feet can be registered.)

   Motor homes 6 - 14 feet, $54.
   Motor homes 15 feet, $163.50. Add $7.50 for each additional foot. (No vehicle over 45 feet can be registered.)

Annual Vehicle Tax .... No
   No property tax on vehicles.

State Emissions Test Required .... Yes
   Within and near the Medford or Portland-Metro areas only. Diesel powered vehicles 8,501 lbs or more are exempt. Web Site: www.deq.state.or.us/aq/vip

Vehicle Safety Inspection Required .... No

Mandatory Minimum Liability Insurance 25/50/20
   Personal Injury Protection and Uninsured Motorist coverage is also required.

VEHICLES

Every state will have some basic fees when you first register a vehicle. Some are a one-time fee and include charges for a title transfer, license plate, plus a myriad of other miscellaneous fees that vary by state. Since these fees are due in every state and the difference between the states is relatively small, they are not included in this guide. As a general rule you can expect to pay about $40 to $100 to cover these expenses.

Registration Fee & Annual Vehicle Tax

The registration fee and annual vehicle tax varies substantially between the states. The basic registration fee is usually higher in states that do not have some form of a vehicle tax. If applicable, the vehicle tax is usually due at the time of registration.

The annual vehicle tax that is imposed by 30 states is basically a personal property tax although they may call it by another name. The fee is usually prorated the first time you register and annually thereafter.

Some states use a simple flat fee while others use a more complicated method which usually takes into account the age, weight, type and value of the vehicle. Where possible, these fees are included. Some rates vary depending on the county you live in or other factors that make it impossible to list the total. Some states provide a "Rate Calculator" at their web site.

These fees and taxes can add up. Once you have narrowed your home base search, you are strongly encouraged to contact the state for estimates on these annual vehicle expenses. Better safe than sorry.

State Emissions Test

There are currently 33 states with an emissions test program. A few are required on a statewide basis but most only require testing in the major metro areas. The rules vary greatly by state and there are usually many exceptions to the rules including type, weight, and age of vehicle. Diesel-powered vehicles are often exempt. Fees for emissions test are generally inexpensive but there can be exceptions. There is also the obvious added expense for repairs if your vehicle fails to pass.

Vehicle Safety Inspection

Twenty states currently require a vehicle safety inspection to verify the vehicle is road worthy. This inspection may be required on an annual basis. There is usually a minimal charge for the inspection.

In most states you will also need to have the vehicle inspected if moving in from another state. This generally is to verify the vehicle identification number. This is usually done free of charge and only when the vehicle is being registered for the first time.

Mandatory Liability Insurance

All states require that you have insurance or proof of financial responsibility before you are allowed to license and register a vehicle. Each state has established minimums that are indicated here.

The actual wording used by each state to define the limits vary. For comparison reasons we have adopted a "general definition" to represent each part of the insurance requirements. Use this as a guide for comparison purposes only.

As an example, the state minimums are represented as: 15/30/10. The general definition used for each number is as follows:

- The first number, 15 ($15,000) is what insurance will pay out *per person* injured in an accident.

- The second number, 30 ($30,000) is tied into the first and reflects the total injury payout *per accident*.

- The third number, 10 (10,000) refers solely to property damage and how much *per accident* the insurance will cover.

In addition to liability insurance, some states require other forms of coverage like Personal Injury Protection, Uninsured Motorist or other forms of "no-fault" coverage.

Note: The only accurate way to determine what your insurance will cost is to speak with an insurance agency in the area you are considering. No matter what type of insurance (health, life, vehicle, etc.) you will want to check the rates for all your insurance needs. The rates do vary greatly by state and location within the state as well as for the type of insurance.

COST OF LIVING INDICATORS
Rank: 1 highest; 51 lowest

Cost of Living - average statewide (rank)	07
Per Capita Income (rank / $)	07 / 48,076
Median Household Income (rank / $)	18 / 55,980
Median House Value (rank / $)	07 / 311,700
Median Property Tax on Homes (rank)	04
Fuel - avg per gal $, Mar 2010 (diesel / gas)	3.12 / 2.87
Fuel Taxes - per gallon $ (diesel / gas)	0.478 / 0.436

Local sales tax can add about 20 cents.

Cigarette Tax - pack of 20 ($)	3.76

New York City adds an additional $1.50.

Tax Burden - average all taxes (rank)	02

COST OF LIVING INDICATORS

In this section you will find values represented in terms of dollars ($) or a rank of 1 through 51 (includes the District of Columbia). The data will help give you a broad overview of economic conditions and is intended for general reference only.

Cost of Living - average statewide

The ranking provided can give you some insight on the average overall costs associated with living in one state compared to another. Obviously many factors can contribute to your living expenses and each individual situation will be different.

Per Capita Income

This shows you in dollar amount and rank the average per capita income.

Median Household Income

Shown is the dollar amount and rank for the median income by household.

Median House Value

This shows the statewide median house value and rank compared to other states. As in all states, homes in rural areas are usually less expensive than in metro areas. It's all about location, location, location.

Median Property Tax on Homes

Property taxes can be a major expense in some states. As with all taxes, rules and rates vary widely by state and even within a state. The amount of taxes collected across the country ranges from about $1.40 to over $17.00 per $1,000 of home value. Use the rank indicated to compare one state with another.

Fuel - average per gallon price

Shown is the average price for both gasoline and diesel fuel. This was in March, 2010, when oil was in the range of $80 per barrel. The averages for all states ranged from $2.67 in Oklahoma to $3.93 in Hawaii for diesel and $2.51 in Missouri to $3.46 in Hawaii for gasoline.

Fuel Taxes - per gallon

The figures shown reflect the fees for state and federal taxes. The federal fee is the same nationwide at 24.4 cents per gallon for diesel and 18.4 cents per gallon for gasoline. The total shown does not include other fees that may be imposed such as state or local sales tax. The averages for all states ranged from 32.4 cents per gallon in Alaska to 69.5 cents per gallon in Connecticut for diesel and 26.4 cents per gallon in Alaska to 60.3 cents per gallon in Connecticut for gasoline.

Cigarette Tax

Amount shown reflects the combined state and federal taxes on a pack of 20 cigarettes. The amount states add to a pack of smokes varies widely. The federal tax is $1.01 per pack nationwide. Local taxes can add even more.

Tax Burden

Use the tax burden rank to compare by state the overall average burden of taxes. This represents income taxes, property taxes, sales taxes, fuel taxes, plus other miscellaneous taxes. Your actual taxes will, of course, vary with your property value, where you live within the state, and your total amount and source of income, among other factors. The overall tax burden across the country represents about 6% to 12% of per capita income. New Jersey ranks #1; Alaska has the lowest burden.

STATE & LOCAL REVENUE SOURCES

Rank: 1 highest; 51 lowest
Rank and % of total revenue from:

Tax Revenue (see "Details" listed below)	48 / 33.08
Charges & Misc. Revenue	07 / 25.18
Federal Government	14 / 19.23
Utility Revenue	08 / 06.37
Insurance Trust Revenue	26 / 16.13

Tax Revenue Details (rank / %)

Property Tax	47 / 15.57
Sales & Gross Receipts	11 / 47.73
Individual Income Tax	31 / 22.70
Corporate Income Tax	29 / 03.76
Motor Vehicle License	23 / 01.70
Other Taxes	18 / 08.54

STATE & LOCAL REVENUE SOURCES

Part One

Part one shows the percentage of income, by source, for combined state and local revenue.

Tax Revenue

Revenue from taxes is probably the one source of state income that effects our wallet the most, at least in a direct manner. Mississippi has the lowest overall total of revenue derived from taxes at 29.50%. Connecticut has the largest percentage at 56.88%. See *Part Two* below for more details.

Charges & Misc. Revenue

This group of state income is from sources like parking facilities, parks and recreation, natural resources, highways, airports, education, interest earnings and other general revenue. Connecticut comes in the lowest at 12.85% and Alaska tops the chart with 35.50%.

Federal Government

This is money given to the states from the federal government. Virginia receives the least at 10.61% and Mississippi has top honors with 33.06%.

Utility Revenue

This represents revenue obtained from water, electric, gas, and transit. At 0.87% New Hampshire receives the least of their total revenue from this source. Nebraska is at the top of the chart with 15.92%.

Insurance Trust Revenue

This income group is comprised of unemployment compensation, employee retirement, worker's compensation, and other insurance trust revenue. The District of Columbia comes in at 7.28% while Oregon is the highest at 31.63%.

Part Two

Part two "Tax Revenue Details" expands on the revenue collected from taxes and provides a break down by the type of tax.

Property Tax

Property tax, usually from real estate, is a major source of income for many states. New Hampshire leads the pack with 61.39% of their tax revenue coming from property tax. New Mexico is the lowest at 13.54%.

Sales & Gross Receipts

This income group includes general sales tax, gross receipts tax, and excise taxes added to items like fuel, alcoholic beverages, and tobacco products. The percent of total revenue collected ranges from 8.67% (OR) to 62.05% (WA).

Individual Income Tax

The individual income tax is another large source of revenue for many of the 43 states with this tax. The amount ranges from 2.27% for New Hampshire to 44.02% in Oregon.

Corporate Income Tax

Although consumers do not pay the Corporate Income Tax directly, it is a cost of doing business for the company and is reflected in the prices paid for their products and services. Hawaii comes in with the lowest percentage of total tax revenue at 1.54%, Alaska is the highest at 16.44%. Four states (NV, TX, WA, and WY) don't have corporate income tax.

Motor Vehicle License and Other Taxes

Motor Vehicle License fees are a small part of each state's total tax revenue. The percentages range from 0.50% in the District of Columbia to 5.12% in Oklahoma.

Other Taxes range from 2.28% to 51.35%. Although 47 states including the District of Columbia are under 15% the remaining four states range from 18.45% in North Dakota to 51.35% in Alaska.

POPULATION

Rank: 1 highest; 51 lowest

State Population (rank / count) .... 14 / 6,595,778
Population Per Square Mile (rank / count) .... 34 / 58

POPULATION

Here you will find the total estimated population for the state and its rank. To put it in perspective, we have also included the population per square mile.

VOTING

Registration Requirements: In-person registration deadline is 29 days before election.

Address Requirements: Physical/street address required.

Register by Mail: Yes, registration deadline is 29 days before election.

Absentee Voting: Yes, no excuse is required. Voters may also place themselves on a "permanent absentee" list.

Web Site: www.elections.colorado.gov

VOTING

In this section you will find pertinent information about the basic rules for voting in a state. The information includes registration and address requirements, registering by mail, and absentee voting. The official web site is also provided for more detailed information.

RESOURCES

Alaska State Government
Phone: 907-465-2200
Web Site: www.state.ak.us

Alaska Department of Revenue
Phone: 907-465-2300
Web Site: www.revenue.state.ak.us

Alaska Division of Motor Vehicles
Phone: 907-269-5551
Web Site: www.state.ak.us/dmv

Alaska Office of Tourism
Phone: 800-862-5275
Web Site: www.travelalaska.com

RESOURCES

Provides official state sources on the Internet for more in-depth information.

AT-A-GLANCE CHARTS

In the back of the book, following the information for Wyoming, you will find 10 charts that will help you easily compare various information by state. Chart categories include:

- State Income Tax
- State and Local Sales Tax
- Fuel Price and Tax
- State Deductions for Pension Income
- Vehicles
- State & Local Revenue Sources
- Cost of Living Indicators

Alabama

WEATHER

	Huntsville			Mobile		
	🌡	💧	❄	🌡	💧	❄
Jan	49/31	5	1.5	61/39	5	0.1
Feb	55/34	5	0.7	65/42	5.2	0.2
Mar	63/41	6.6	0.4	71/49	6.6	0.1
Apr	72/48	4.8	0	77/55	5.3	0
May	80/57	5.1	0	84/63	5.6	0
Jun	87/65	4.3	0	89/69	5.3	0
Jul	89/70	4.6	0	91/72	7.7	0
Aug	89/68	3.5	0	91/72	6.8	0
Sep	83/62	4.1	0	87/68	6	0
Oct	73/50	3.3	0	79/56	3	0
Nov	62/41	4.7	0	70/48	4.2	0
Dec	52/34	5.7	0.2	63/42	5.4	0.1

🌡	Average monthly high and low temperatures in degrees Fahrenheit.
💧	Average monthly precipitation totals in inches.
❄	Average monthly snowfall totals in inches.

STATE AND LOCAL TAXES

State Sales Tax (%) 4.00
  Exempt: prescription drugs.

Local Sales Taxes (up to an additional %) 8.00
Inheritance Tax .... No
Estate Tax...Yes
  Limited to federal estate tax collection

PERSONAL INCOME TAXES

State Income Tax (%) ....2 - 5
  3 income brackets - Lowest $500; Highest $3,000. City and/or county income taxes not included.

Personal Exemption $ (single / joint) ....1,500 / 3,000
Standard Deduction $ (single / joint)............2,000 / 4,000
Federal Income Tax Paid - Deduction Allowed ....Full
Social Security Income - Tax Exempt.................................Yes
Retired Military Pay - Tax Exempt ....Yes
State & Local Government Pensions - Tax Exempt ....Yes

Federal Civil Service Pensions - Tax Exempt ....Yes
Railroad Retirement - Tax Exempt ....Yes
Private Pension - Tax Exempt ....Limits
  Exempt for qualified plans.

VEHICLES

Registration Fees .... 1 Year
  Passenger cars and pickups to 8,000 lbs GVW, $23.
  Travel trailers, $12.
  Motor home fees are based on GVW:
  0 - 8,000 lbs, $23.
  8,001 - 12,000 lbs, $50.
  12,001 - 18,000 lbs, $100.
  18,001 - 26,000 lbs, $175.
  26,001 - 33,000 lbs, $275.
  33,001 - 42,000 lbs, $500.
  Over 42,000 lbs, varies.

Annual Vehicle Tax ....Yes
  Annual property tax on vehicles.

State Emissions Test Required .... No
Vehicle Safety Inspection Required .... No
Mandatory Minimum Liability Insurance 25/50/25

COST OF LIVING INDICATORS

  Rank: 1 highest; 51 lowest

Cost of Living - average statewide (rank) 41
Per Capita Income (rank / $) ....42 / 33,643
Median Household Income (rank / $) ....47 / 42,586
Median House Value (rank / $)........................45 / 114,700
Median Property Tax on Homes (rank) 50
Fuel - avg per gal $, Mar 2010 (diesel / gas).....2.79 / 2.63
Fuel Taxes - per gallon $ (diesel / gas)...........0.444 / 0.374
  Local taxes may add up to 3 cents.
Cigarette Tax - pack of 20 ($) 1.44
Tax Burden - average all taxes (rank)................................. 39

STATE & LOCAL REVENUE SOURCES

  Rank: 1 highest; 51 lowest
  Rank and % of total revenue from:

Tax Revenue (see "Details" listed below)............48 / 33.08
Charges & Misc. Revenue..07 / 25.18
Federal Government ....14 / 19.23
Utility Revenue ....08 / 06.37
Insurance Trust Revenue..26 / 16.13

  Tax Revenue Details (rank / %)

Property Tax...47 / 15.57
Sales & Gross Receipts ....11 / 47.73

Individual Income Tax...31 / 22.70
Corporate Income Tax..29 / 03.76
Motor Vehicle License...23 / 01.70
Other Taxes...18 / 08.54

POPULATION

Rank: 1 highest; 51 lowest

State Population (rank / count) ....23 / 4,708,708
Population Per Square Mile (rank / count) ....26 / 90

VOTING

Registration Requirements: In-person registration deadline is 11 days before election.

Address Requirements: Physical/street address required.

Register by Mail: Yes, registration deadline is 11 days before election.

Absentee Voting: Yes, excuse required. Absentee voting application deadline is five days prior to election.

Web Site: www.sos.state.al.us/Elections/

RESOURCES

Alabama State Government
Phone: 334-242-8000
Web Site: www.alabama.gov

Alabama Department of Revenue
Phone: 334-242-1170
Web Site: www.ador.state.al.us

Alabama Motor Vehicles Division
Phone: 334-242-9000
Web Site: www.ador.state.al.us/motorvehicle/index.html

Alabama Office of Tourism
Phone: 800-Alabama
Web Site: www.800alabama.com

Alaska

WEATHER

	Anchorage			Juneau		
	🌡	💧	❄	🌡	💧	❄
Jan	22/8	0.8	10.7	29/18	4.2	26
Feb	25/11	0.8	11.5	34/22	3.7	19
Mar	33/17	0.7	9	39/26	3.3	14.9
Apr	43/28	0.6	4.8	47/32	2.8	3.5
May	55/39	0.7	0.4	55/39	3.5	0
Jun	62/47	1	0	61/45	3	0
Jul	65/51	1.9	0	64/48	4.2	0
Aug	63/49	2.4	0	63/47	5.1	0
Sep	55/41	2.7	0.3	56/43	7.1	0
Oct	41/28	1.9	7.3	47/37	7.7	1.1
Nov	28/15	1.1	10.7	37/28	5.7	11.9
Dec	22/10	1.1	14.8	32/23	4.8	22.6
🌡	Average monthly high and low temperatures in degrees Fahrenheit.					
💧	Average monthly precipitation totals in inches.					
❄	Average monthly snowfall totals in inches.					

STATE AND LOCAL TAXES

State Sales Tax (%) .... None
Local Sales Taxes (up to an additional %) 7.00
Inheritance Tax .... No
Estate Tax...Yes
Limited to federal estate tax collection.

PERSONAL INCOME TAXES

State Income Tax (%) .... None
Personal Exemption $ (single / joint) .... n/a
Standard Deduction $ (single / joint)................................ n/a
Federal Income Tax Paid - Deduction Allowed .... n/a
Social Security Income - Tax Exempt................................. n/a
Retired Military Pay - Tax Exempt .... n/a
State & Local Government Pensions - Tax Exempt .... n/a
Federal Civil Service Pensions - Tax Exempt .... n/a
Railroad Retirement - Tax Exempt .... n/a
Private Pension - Tax Exempt .... n/a

VEHICLES

Registration Fees .... 2 Years
Passenger vehicles and motor homes, $100.
Trucks and cargo vans under 10,000 lbs, $100.
Trailers, $30.

Annual Vehicle Tax ....Yes
Some municipalities and boroughs levy a Motor Vehicle
Registration Tax.

State Emissions Test Required ....Yes
For Municipality of Anchorage. New vehicles are exempt
for the first six years. Vehicles powered by diesel are
subject to a one-time inspection, per owner. Vehicles
with an empty weight over 12,000 lbs are exempt.
Web Site: http://state.ak.us/dmv/reg/imtest.htm

Vehicle Safety Inspection Required .... No
Mandatory Minimum Liability Insurance 50/100/25

COST OF LIVING INDICATORS

Rank: 1 highest; 51 lowest

Cost of Living - average statewide (rank) 04
Per Capita Income (rank / $) ....08 / 43,321
Median Household Income (rank / $) ....04 / 67,332
Median House Value (rank / $)..........................18 / 226,900
Median Property Tax on Homes (rank) 13
Fuel - avg per gal $, Mar 2010 (diesel / gas).....3.60 / 3.38
Fuel Taxes - per gallon $ (diesel / gas)............0.324 / 0.264
Cigarette Tax - pack of 20 ($) 3.01
Plus $1.45 in Anchorage, $1 in Barrow, Sitka or Juneau,
and 20 cents in Fairbanks.
Tax Burden - average all taxes (rank)..................................51

STATE & LOCAL REVENUE SOURCES

Rank: 1 highest; 51 lowest
Rank and % of total revenue from:

Tax Revenue (see "Details" listed below) ....49 / 32.00
Charges & Misc. Revenue...01 / 35.51
Federal Government ....26 / 16.47
Utility Revenue ....37 / 01.95
Insurance Trust Revenue...34 / 14.07

Tax Revenue Details (rank / %)

Property Tax..42 / 20.95
Sales & Gross Receipts ....50 / 09.85
Individual Income Tax..44 / 0
Corporate Income Tax..01 / 16.44
Motor Vehicle License..31 / 01.41
Other Taxes ....01 / 51.35

POPULATION

Rank: 1 highest; 51 lowest

State Population (rank / count) ....47 / 698,473
Population Per Square Mile (rank / count) ....51 / 1

VOTING

Registration Requirements: In-person registration
deadline is 30 days before election.

Address Requirements: Physical/street address required.

Register by Mail: Yes, registration deadline is 30 days
before election.

Absentee Voting: Yes, no excuse is required.

Web Site: www.elections.alaska.gov/

RESOURCES

Alaska State Government
Phone: 907-465-2200
Web Site: www.state.ak.us

Alaska Department of Revenue
Phone: 907-465-2300
Web Site: www.revenue.state.ak.us

Alaska Division of Motor Vehicles
Phone: 907-269-5551
Web Site: www.state.ak.us/dmv

Alaska Office of Tourism
Phone: 800-862-5275
Web Site: www.travelalaska.com

Arizona

WEATHER

	Flagstaff			Phoenix		
	🌡	💧	❄	🌡	💧	❄
Jan	42/15	2.1	20.7	66/41	0.8	N/A
Feb	45/18	2.2	18.3	70/44	0.6	N/A
Mar	49/22	2.4	22.3	75/49	0.9	N/A
Apr	58/27	1.3	9.5	84/55	0.3	N/A
May	67/34	0.8	1.8	93/64	0.1	N/A
Jun	78/41	0.5	0	103/72	0.1	N/A
Jul	82/50	2.5	0	105/80	0.8	N/A
Aug	79/49	2.9	0	103/79	1	N/A
Sep	74/41	1.8	0.1	99/72	0.7	N/A
Oct	64/31	1.6	2	88/61	0.6	N/A
Nov	51/22	1.8	10.2	75/48	0.6	N/A
Dec	44/16	2.1	15.9	66/42	0.9	N/A

🌡	Average monthly high and low temperatures in degrees Fahrenheit.
💧	Average monthly precipitation totals in inches.
❄	Average monthly snowfall totals in inches.

STATE AND LOCAL TAXES

State Sales Tax (%) ....See note
Arizona has a Transaction Privilege Tax (TPT) with various rates. The tax is levied on the vender which is usually passed on to the consumer. Common retail transactions run about 6.3%. Exempt: food and prescription drugs.

Local Sales Taxes (up to an additional %) ....See note
All fifteen counties levy a tax ranging from 0.5% to 1.125%. Cities may also levy a sales tax.

Inheritance Tax .... No
Estate Tax.. No

PERSONAL INCOME TAXES

State Income Tax (%) ....2.59 - 4.54
5 income brackets - Lowest $10,000; Highest $150,000.

Personal Exemption $ (single / joint) ....2,100 / 4,200
Standard Deduction $ (single / joint)............4,677 / 9,354
Federal Income Tax Paid - Deduction Allowed .... None

Social Security Income - Tax Exempt................................Yes
Retired Military Pay - Tax Exempt ....Limits
Up to $2,500 exempt.

State & Local Government Pensions - Tax Exempt .. Limits
Up to $2,500 exempt.

Federal Civil Service Pensions - Tax Exempt ....Limits
Up to $2,500 exempt.

Railroad Retirement - Tax Exempt ....Yes
Private Pension - Tax Exempt .... No

VEHICLES

Registration Fees .... 1 Year
Basic fee, $13.50. The VLT tax described below will be in addition to the basic fee.

Annual Vehicle Tax ....Yes
An annual vehicle license tax (VLT) assessed in place of property tax. VLT is based on an assessed value of 60% of the manufacturer's base retail price reduced by 16.25% for each year since the vehicle was first registered in Arizona. The rate is calculated as $2.80 (new vehicles) or $2.89 (used vehicles) for each $100 of the assessed value.

Example: A new vehicle that costs $25,000, the first year assessed value is $15,000 and the VLT would be $420. The second year VLT would be $363.06.

State Emissions Test Required ....Yes
In metro Phoenix and Tucson emission test areas. Some exceptions.
Web Site: www.azdeq.gov/environ/air/vei/index.html.

Vehicle Safety Inspection Required .... No
Mandatory Minimum Liability Insurance 15/30/10

COST OF LIVING INDICATORS

Rank: 1 highest; 51 lowest

Cost of Living - average statewide (rank) 16
Per Capita Income (rank / $) ....43 / 32,953
Median Household Income (rank / $) ....23 / 51,009
Median House Value (rank / $)..........................17 / 234,600
Median Property Tax on Homes (rank) 34
Fuel - avg per gal $, Mar 2010 (diesel / gas).....2.90 / 2.67
Fuel Taxes - per gallon $ (diesel / gas)...........0.434 / 0.374
Cigarette Tax - pack of 20 ($) 3.01
Tax Burden - average all taxes (rank) 42

STATE & LOCAL REVENUE SOURCES

Rank: 1 highest; 51 lowest
Rank and % of total revenue from:

Tax Revenue (see "Details" listed below) ....14 / 45.41
Charges & Misc. Revenue................................37 / 18.04
Federal Government ....22 / 16.96
Utility Revenue...04 / 07.75
Insurance Trust Revenue................................45 / 11.84

Tax Revenue Details (rank / %)

Property Tax..33 / 26.66
Sales & Gross Receipts ....09 / 48.42
Individual Income Tax....................................38 / 16.06
Corporate Income Tax...................................25 / 04.23
Motor Vehicle License...................................37 / 01.02
Other Taxes ....40 / 03.61

POPULATION

Rank: 1 highest; 51 lowest

State Population (rank / count) .... 14 / 6,595,778
Population Per Square Mile (rank / count) .... 34 / 58

VOTING

Registration Requirements: In-person registration deadline is 29 days before election.

Address Requirements: Physical/street address required.

Register by Mail: Yes, registration deadline is 29 days before election.

Absentee Voting: Yes, no excuse is required.

Web Site: www.azsos.gov/election/

RESOURCES

Arizona State Government
Phone: 602-542-4900
Web Site: www.az.gov

Arizona Department of Revenue
Phone: 602-255-3381
Web Site: www.azdor.gov

Arizona Motor Vehicle Division
Phone: 800-251-5866
Web Site: www.azdot.gov/mvd

Arizona Office of Tourism
Phone: 866-275-5816
Web Site: www.arizonaguide.com

Arkansas

WEATHER

	Little Rock			Texarkana		
	🌡	💧	❄	🌡	💧	❄
Jan	50/31	4.1	2.3	57/36	5	1.4
Feb	55/34	4	1.4	60/38	3.7	0.2
Mar	63/42	4.8	0.5	67/44	4.1	0
Apr	73/51	5.3	0	76/52	5.7	0
May	81/60	5.2	0	83/61	4.1	0
Jun	89/68	3.6	0	91/69	4	0
Jul	92/72	3.5	0	94/72	4.1	0
Aug	92/70	3.2	0	95/71	3	0
Sep	85/63	3.8	0	90/65	2.6	0
Oct	75/51	3.6	0	80/54	2.9	0
Nov	62/41	4.9	0.2	66/42	4.3	0
Dec	53/34	4.4	0.7	58/38	4.7	0

🌡	Average monthly high and low temperatures in degrees Fahrenheit.
💧	Average monthly precipitation totals in inches.
❄	Average monthly snowfall totals in inches.

STATE AND LOCAL TAXES

State Sales Tax (%)...6.00
Prescription drugs exempt. Food is taxed at 2%.

Local Sales Taxes (up to an additional %) 6.50
Inheritance Tax .... No
Estate Tax.. No

PERSONAL INCOME TAXES

State Income Tax (%)..1 - 7
6 income brackets - Lowest $3,899; Highest $32,600. City and/or county income taxes not included.

Personal Exemption $ (single / joint) .... 23 / 46
Amount is a tax credit.

Standard Deduction $ (single / joint)............2,000 / 4,000
Federal Income Tax Paid - Deduction Allowed .... None
Social Security Income - Tax Exempt................................Yes
Retired Military Pay - Tax Exempt ....Limits
State & Local Government Pensions - Tax Exempt ..Limits

Federal Civil Service Pensions - Tax Exempt .... Limits
Railroad Retirement - Tax Exempt .... Yes
Private Pension - Tax Exempt .... Limits

Note: Limits include a maximum combined exemption of $6,000 from all retirement income sources other than Social Security and Railroad Retirement.

VEHICLES

Registration Fees .... 1 Year
Passenger cars, trucks, vans, and motor homes. Rate is based on vehicle weight, $20 - $33.
Trailers, for permanent trailer tag, $36.

Annual Vehicle Tax .... Yes
Annual property tax on vehicles.

State Emissions Test Required .... No
Vehicle Safety Inspection Required .... No
Mandatory Minimum Liability Insurance 25/50/25
Personal Injury Protection is also required.

COST OF LIVING INDICATORS

Rank: 1 highest; 51 lowest

Cost of Living - average statewide (rank) 49
Per Capita Income (rank / $) .... 48 / 31,266
Median Household Income (rank / $) .... 49 / 38,820
Median House Value (rank / $) .... 49 / 99,600
Median Property Tax on Homes (rank) 47
Fuel - avg per gal $, Mar 2010 (diesel / gas) ..... 2.77 / 2.59
Fuel Taxes - per gallon $ (diesel / gas) .... 0.472 / 0.402
Cigarette Tax - pack of 20 ($) 2.16
Tax Burden - average all taxes (rank) 15

STATE & LOCAL REVENUE SOURCES

Rank: 1 highest; 51 lowest
Rank and % of total revenue from:

Tax Revenue (see "Details" listed below) .... 27 / 40.72
Charges & Misc. Revenue .... 39 / 17.77
Federal Government .... 12 / 19.99
Utility Revenue .... 23 / 03.52
Insurance Trust Revenue .... 19 / 18.01

Tax Revenue Details (rank / %)

Property Tax .... 50 / 14.69
Sales & Gross Receipts .... 05 / 53.23
Individual Income Tax .... 26 / 23.62
Corporate Income Tax .... 27 / 03.95
Motor Vehicle License .... 30 / 01.43
Other Taxes .... 47 / 03.08

POPULATION

Rank: 1 highest; 51 lowest

State Population (rank / count) .... 32 / 2,889,450
Population Per Square Mile (rank / count) .... 35 / 54

VOTING

Registration Requirements: In-person registration deadline is 30 days before election.

Address Requirements: Physical/street address required.

Register by Mail: Yes, registration deadline is 30 days before election.

Absentee Voting: Yes, no excuse is required. To be qualified to vote an absentee ballot, you must meet one of the following criteria: You will be unavoidably absent from your polling site on election day (the law does not require you to give a reason), or you will be unable to attend the polls on election day because of illness or physical disability.

Web Site: www.votenaturally.org/

RESOURCES

Arkansas State Government
Phone: 501-682-3000
Web Site: www.arkansas.gov

Arkansas Department of Finance and Administration
Phone: 501-682-7225
Web Site: www.arkansas.gov/dfa

Arkansas Office of Motor Vehicle
Phone: 501-682-4692
Web Site: www.dfa.arkansas.gov/offices/motorVehicle/..
     Pages/default.aspx

Arkansas Office of Tourism
Phone: 800-628-8725
Web Site: www.arkansas.com

Moving to Arkansas, A Tax Guide For New Residents
Web Site: www.arkansas.gov/dfa/income_tax/
documents/moving_2_arkansas.pdf

California

WEATHER

	San Francisco			Los Angeles		
	🌡	💧	❄	🌡	💧	❄
Jan	56/46	4.1	N/A	65/48	2.7	N/A
Feb	60/48	3.5	N/A	66/49	3.1	N/A
Mar	61/49	2.9	N/A	68/50	2.2	N/A
Apr	63/50	1.5	N/A	70/53	1.3	N/A
May	64/51	0.5	N/A	73/56	0.3	N/A
Jun	66/53	0.2	N/A	76/58	0.1	N/A
Jul	66/54	0	N/A	82/62	0	N/A
Aug	66/54	0	N/A	82/63	0	N/A
Sep	70/56	0.2	N/A	81/61	0.2	N/A
Oct	69/55	1.1	N/A	77/58	0.4	N/A
Nov	64/51	2.6	N/A	73/53	1.1	N/A
Dec	57/47	3.9	N/A	68/50	2.5	N/A
🌡	Average monthly high and low temperatures in degrees Fahrenheit.					
💧	Average monthly precipitation totals in inches.					
❄	Average monthly snowfall totals in inches.					

STATE AND LOCAL TAXES

State Sales Tax (%) 8.25
Exempt: food and prescription drugs.

Local Sales Taxes (up to an additional %) 2.50

Inheritance Tax .... No

Estate Tax ....Yes
Limited to federal estate tax collection.

PERSONAL INCOME TAXES

State Income Tax (%) .... 1.25 - 10.55
7 income brackets - Lowest $7,168; Highest $1,000,000.

Personal Exemption $ (single / joint) ....99 / 198
Amount is a tax credit.

Standard Deduction $ (single / joint).............3,692 / 7384

Federal Income Tax Paid - Deduction Allowed .... None

Social Security Income - Tax Exempt ....Yes

Retired Military Pay - Tax Exempt .... No

State & Local Government Pensions - Tax Exempt .... No

Federal Civil Service Pensions - Tax Exempt .... No

Railroad Retirement - Tax Exempt ....Yes

Private Pension - Tax Exempt .... No

VEHICLES

Registration Fees .... 1 Year
$ 55 plus. Fees vary. An exact amount can only be calculated when you submit your application. Some fees are due on every vehicle, assessment of other fees is based on type of vehicle and county of residence.

To estimate registration fees you can use the "Vehicle Registration Fee Calculator" at https://mv.dmv.ca.gov/ FeeCalculatorWeb/newResidentForm.do

In addition to registration fees, a Nonresident Service Fee of $17 is charged for any vehicle previously registered out-of-state.

Annual Vehicle Tax ....Yes
An annual Vehicle License Fee (VLF) is assessed in lieu of property tax. The VLF is based on the purchase price or the value of the vehicle when acquired. The VLF decreases with each renewal for the first 11 years.

State Emissions Test Required ....Yes
Every two years in 40 counties (only some "Zip Codes" within 6 of the counties). Diesel powdered vehicles manufactured prior to 1998 or with a GVWR of more than 14,000 lbs are exempt.
Web Site: www.dmv.ca.gov/vr/smogfaq.htm

Vehicle Safety Inspection Required .... No

Mandatory Minimum Liability Insurance 15/30/5

COST OF LIVING INDICATORS
Rank: 1 highest; 51 lowest

Cost of Living - average statewide (rank) 03

Per Capita Income (rank / $) .... 12 / 42,696

Median Household Income (rank / $) .... 09 / 61,017

Median House Value (rank / $)..........................02 / 510,200

Median Property Tax on Homes (rank) 10

Fuel - avg per gal $, Mar 2010 (diesel / gas) .....3.09 / 3.01

Fuel Taxes - per gallon $ (diesel / gas)...........0.438 / 0.378
Plus state and local sales taxes.

Cigarette Tax - pack of 20 ($) 1.88

Tax Burden - average all taxes (rank) 06

STATE & LOCAL REVENUE SOURCES
Rank: 1 highest; 51 lowest
Rank and % of total revenue from:

Tax Revenue (see "Details" listed below) ....42 / 36.99
Charges & Misc. Revenue................................41 / 17.48
Federal Government ....49 / 11.84
Utility Revenue..10 / 05.51
Insurance Trust Revenue..............................02 / 28.19

Tax Revenue Details (rank / %)

Property Tax...37 / 24.13
Sales & Gross Receipts ....33 / 31.35
Individual Income Tax..................................07 / 30.83
Corporate Income Tax..................................09 / 06.45
Motor Vehicle License..................................28 / 01.53
Other Taxes ....25 / 05.71

POPULATION

Rank: 1 highest; 51 lowest

State Population (rank / count) ....01 / 36,961,664
Population Per Square Mile (rank / count) ....12 / 226

VOTING

Registration Requirements: In-person registration deadline is 15 days before election.

Address Requirements: Physical/street address required.

Register by Mail: Yes, registration deadline is 15 days before election.

Absentee Voting: Yes, no excuse is required. Voters may also place themselves on a "permanent absentee" list.

Web Site: www.sos.ca.gov/elections/

RESOURCES

California State Government
Phone: 916-657-9900
Web Site: www.ca.gov

California Franchise Tax Board
Phone: 800-338-0505
Web Site: www.taxes.ca.gov

California Department of Motor Vehicles
Phone: 800-777-0133
Web Site: www.dmv.ca.gov

California Office of Tourism
Phone: 800-862-2543
Web Site: www.gocalif.ca.gov

Colorado

WEATHER

	Denver			Pueblo		
	🌡	💧	❄	🌡	💧	❄
Jan	43/16	0.5	8.2	45/14	0.3	5.9
Feb	47/20	0.6	7.4	50/19	0.3	4.3
Mar	52/26	1.3	12.6	57/26	0.8	6.9
Apr	62/35	1.8	8.9	67/35	1	3.5
May	71/44	2.5	1.6	76/46	1.5	0.7
Jun	82/53	1.7	0	87/54	1.3	0
Jul	88/59	1.9	0	92/60	1.9	0
Aug	86/57	1.5	0	90/59	2.1	0
Sep	77/48	1.1	1.6	81/50	0.9	0.5
Oct	66/37	1	3.8	70/36	0.8	1.3
Nov	52/25	0.9	8.9	56/24	0.5	4.6
Dec	45/18	0.6	7.4	47/16	0.4	5.3
🌡	Average monthly high and low temperatures in degrees Fahrenheit.					
💧	Average monthly precipitation totals in inches.					
❄	Average monthly snowfall totals in inches.					

STATE AND LOCAL TAXES

State Sales Tax (%) 2.90
Exempt: food and prescription drugs.

Local Sales Taxes (up to an additional %) 7.00
Inheritance Tax .... No
Estate Tax.. No

PERSONAL INCOME TAXES

State Income Tax (%) 4.63
Flat rate, no income brackets.

Personal Exemption $ (single / joint) ....3,650 / 7,300
Standard Deduction $ (single / joint)........................... None
Federal Income Tax Paid - Deduction Allowed.......... None
Social Security Income - Tax Exempt.................................Yes
Retired Military Pay - Tax Exempt ....Limits
State & Local Government Pensions - Tax Exempt..Limits
Federal Civil Service Pensions - Tax Exempt ....Limits
Railroad Retirement - Tax Exempt ....Yes

Private Pension - Tax Exempt .... Limits

Note: Limits include a maximum combined exemption of $20,000 ($24,000 if 65 or older) from all retirement income sources other than Social Security and Railroad Retirement.

VEHICLES

Registration Fees .... 1 Year
Fees vary by county and are based on age of the vehicle, weight, taxable value, and purchase date. Estimates are not available over the phone.

Some county web sites will help calculate the fees, visit www.ccionline.org/ for a list of Colorado counties. If the fees are not available on the county web site you will need to go to the county motor vehicle office.

Annual Vehicle Tax ....Yes
An annual "Ownership Tax" is assessed in lieu of property tax.

State Emissions Test Required ....Yes
In some counties, especially around Denver. Requirements for gasoline and diesel powered vehicles vary by county. Web Site: www.aircarecolorado.com

Vehicle Safety Inspection Required .... No
Mandatory Minimum Liability Insurance 25/50/15

COST OF LIVING INDICATORS
Rank: 1 highest; 51 lowest

Cost of Living - average statewide (rank) 17
Per Capita Income (rank / $) .... 14 / 42,377
Median Household Income (rank / $) .... 14 / 57,184
Median House Value (rank / $) ....16 / 236,300
Median Property Tax on Homes (rank) 31
Fuel - avg per gal $, Mar 2010 (diesel / gas) ......2.80 / 2.59
Fuel Taxes - per gallon $ (diesel / gas) ....0.449 / 0.404
Cigarette Tax - pack of 20 ($) 1.84
Tax Burden - average all taxes (rank) 35

STATE & LOCAL REVENUE SOURCES
Rank: 1 highest; 51 lowest
Rank and % of total revenue from:

Tax Revenue (see "Details" listed below) ....30 / 39.83
Charges & Misc. Revenue ....12 / 23.63
Federal Government ....48 / 12.22
Utility Revenue ....15 / 04.67
Insurance Trust Revenue ....14 / 19.64

Tax Revenue Details (rank / %)
Property Tax ....22 / 30.38
Sales & Gross Receipts ....23 / 35.39
Individual Income Tax ....18 / 25.74
Corporate Income Tax ....42 / 02.57
Motor Vehicle License ....32 / 01.39
Other Taxes ....34 / 04.53

POPULATION
Rank: 1 highest; 51 lowest

State Population (rank / count) .... 22 / 5,024,748
Population Per Square Mile (rank / count) .... 38 / 48

VOTING

Registration Requirements: In-person registration deadline is 29 days before election.

Address Requirements: Physical/street address required.

Register by Mail: Yes, registration deadline is 29 days before election.

Absentee Voting: Yes, no excuse is required. Voters may also place themselves on a "permanent absentee" list.

Web Site: www.elections.colorado.gov/

RESOURCES

Colorado State Government
Phone: 800-970-3468
Web Site: www.colorado.gov

Colorado Department of Revenue
Phone: 303-238-7378
Web Site: www.revenue.state.co.us

Colorado Division of Motor Vehicles
Phone: 303-205-5600
Web Site: www.colorado.gov/revenue/dmv

Colorado Office of Tourism
Phone: 800-265-6723
Web Site: www.colorado.com

Connecticut

WEATHER

	Bridgeport			Hartford		
	🌡	💧	❄	🌡	💧	❄
Jan	37/23	3.2	7.3	34/17	3.4	12
Feb	38/24	2.9	7.3	37/19	3.1	11.4
Mar	46/31	3.8	4.8	46/28	3.9	9.9
Apr	57/40	3.7	0.4	60/38	3.9	1.6
May	67/50	3.6	0	71/47	3.7	0
Jun	77/59	3	0	80/57	3.5	0
Jul	82/66	3.5	0	85/62	3.3	0
Aug	81/65	3.8	0	82/60	4	0
Sep	74/57	3.1	0	74/52	3.8	0
Oct	64/47	3.2	0	64/41	3.6	0.1
Nov	53/38	3.8	0.6	51/33	4.1	2
Dec	41/27	3.5	4.5	38/22	3.9	10.3

🌡	Average monthly high and low temperatures in degrees Fahrenheit.
💧	Average monthly precipitation totals in inches.
❄	Average monthly snowfall totals in inches.

STATE AND LOCAL TAXES

State Sales Tax (%)...6.00
  Exempt: food and prescription drugs.

Local Sales Taxes (up to an additional %) .... None
Inheritance Tax ....Yes
  A spouse is exempt from the tax.

Estate Tax..Yes
  On estates valued at $3.5 million or more.

PERSONAL INCOME TAXES

State Income Tax (%) .... 3 - 6.5
  3 income brackets - Lowest, first $10,000; Highest, over $500,000.

Personal Exemption $ (single / joint) ....13,000 / 24,000
  There is a $1,000 reduction in the exemption amount for every $1,000 of state adjusted gross income over 26,000 for single filers and $48,000 on joint returns.

Standard Deduction $ (single / joint)...........................None
Federal Income Tax Paid - Deduction Allowed ....None
Social Security Income - Tax Exempt...........................Limits
  Exempt for individual taxpayers with federal adjusted gross income of less than $50,000. Married, joint return $60,000.

Retired Military Pay - Tax Exempt ....Limits
  50% is tax exempt.

State & Local Government Pensions - Tax Exempt .... No
Federal Civil Service Pensions - Tax Exempt .... No
Railroad Retirement - Tax Exempt ....Yes
Private Pension - Tax Exempt .... No

VEHICLES

Registration Fees .... 2 Years
  Passenger vehicle, $75.
  Trucks and sport utility vehicles are based on the GVWR of the vehicle:
  less than 5,000 lbs, $81 - $129.
  5,100 - 8,000 lbs, $152.50 - $198.60.
  8,100 - 10,000 lbs, $200.92 - $245.
  10,100 - 12,500 lbs, $247.32 - $303.
  Camper, $70.

Annual Vehicle Tax ....Yes
  Annual property tax on vehicles.

State Emissions Test Required ....Yes
  Statewide, every two years. Vehicles with a GVWR of more than 10,000 lbs are exempt.
  Web Site: www.ctemissions.com

Vehicle Safety Inspection Required ....Yes
  Some exceptions.

Mandatory Minimum Liability Insurance 20/40/10
  Uninsured and Underinsured Motorists coverage is also required.

COST OF LIVING INDICATORS

  Rank: 1 highest; 51 lowest

Cost of Living - average statewide (rank) 08
Per Capita Income (rank / $) .... 02 / 56,248
Median Household Income (rank / $) ....03 / 68,294
Median House Value (rank / $).........................08 / 305,100
Median Property Tax on Homes (rank) 02
Fuel - avg per gal $, Mar 2010 (diesel / gas).....3.14 / 2.85
Fuel Taxes - per gallon $ (diesel / gas)...........0.695 / 0.603
Cigarette Tax - pack of 20 ($) 4.01
Tax Burden - average all taxes (rank) 03

STATE & LOCAL REVENUE SOURCES

Rank: 1 highest; 51 lowest
Rank and % of total revenue from:

Tax Revenue (see "Details" listed below) ....01 / 56.88
Charges & Misc. Revenue.......................................51 / 12.85
Federal Government ....46 / 12.34
Utility Revenue...37 / 01.95
Insurance Trust Revenue.......................................29 / 15.99

Tax Revenue Details (rank / %)

Property Tax...07 / 38.26
Sales & Gross Receipts ....44 / 23.54
Individual Income Tax..09 / 30.03
Corporate Income Tax..28 / 03.91
Motor Vehicle License..38 / 00.96
Other Taxes ....45 / 03.30

POPULATION

Rank: 1 highest; 51 lowest

State Population (rank / count) ....29 / 3,518,288
Population Per Square Mile (rank / count) ....04 / 635

VOTING

Registration Requirements: In-person registration deadline is 7 days before election.

Address Requirements: Physical/street address required.

Register by Mail: Yes, registration deadline is 14 days before election.

Absentee Voting: Yes, no excuse is required.

Web Site: www.ct.gov/sots/site/

RESOURCES

Connecticut State Government
Phone: 860-622-2200
Web Site: www.ct.gov

Connecticut Department of Revenue Services
Phone: 860-297-5962
Web Site: www.ct.gov/drs

Connecticut Department of Motor Vehicles
Phone: 860-263-5700
Web Site: www.ct.gov/dmv

Connecticut Office of Tourism
Phone: 800-288-4748
Web Site: www.ctvisit.com

Delaware

WEATHER

	Dover			Wilmington		
	🌡	💧	❄	🌡	💧	❄
Jan	44/27	3.4	4.9	40/24	3.1	6.6
Feb	45/27	3.2	5.1	42/25	2.9	6
Mar	54/34	4	2.9	51/33	3.8	3.3
Apr	65/43	3.5	0.5	63/42	3.3	0.2
May	75/53	3.8	0	73/52	3.7	0
Jun	83/62	3.5	0	82/61	3.3	0
Jul	87/67	4.6	0	86/67	4.3	0
Aug	85/65	5.1	0	84/65	3.8	0
Sep	79/59	3.7	0	77/58	3.7	0
Oct	68/48	3	0.1	67/46	2.8	0.1
Nov	57/38	3.3	0.4	55/37	3.3	0.9
Dec	46/29	3.3	3.9	44/27	3.4	3.3
🌡	Average monthly high and low temperatures in degrees Fahrenheit.					
💧	Average monthly precipitation totals in inches.					
❄	Average monthly snowfall totals in inches.					

STATE AND LOCAL TAXES

State Sales Tax (%)..See note
Delaware has a gross receipts tax of 0.104% to 2.07%, depending on the business activity.

Local Sales Taxes (up to an additional %) ....None
Inheritance Tax ....No
Estate Tax..Yes

PERSONAL INCOME TAXES

State Income Tax (%)..2.2 - 6.95
7 income brackets - Lowest $2,000; Highest $60,000. City and/or county income taxes not included.

Personal Exemption $ (single / joint) ....110 / 220
Amount is a tax credit.

Standard Deduction $ (single / joint)............3,250 / 6,500
If not itemizing.

Federal Income Tax Paid - Deduction Allowed .... None
Social Security Income - Tax Exempt.................................Yes

Retired Military Pay - Tax Exempt .... Limits
State & Local Government Pensions - Tax Exempt ..Limits
Federal Civil Service Pensions - Tax Exempt .... Limits
Railroad Retirement - Tax Exempt ....Yes
Private Pension - Tax Exempt .... Limits

Note: Limits include a maximum combined exemption of $2,000 ($12,500 if 60 or older) from all retirement income sources other than Social Security and Railroad Retirement.

VEHICLES

Registration Fees .... 1 Year
Cars, light duty trucks and vans 5,000 lbs or less: $40. Motor homes and travel trailers for the first 5,000 lbs, $40. Additional $6.40 per 1,000 lbs above 5,000 lbs.

Annual Vehicle Tax .... No
No property tax on vehicles.

State Emissions Test Required ....Yes
Annual, diesel fueled vehicles model year 1996 and older are exempt. Web Site: www.dmv.de.gov/services/ vehicle_services/other/ve_other_general.shtml

Vehicle Safety Inspection Required ....Yes
Annual, some exceptions.

Mandatory Minimum Liability Insurance 15/30/10
Personal Injury Protection is also required.

COST OF LIVING INDICATORS

Rank: 1 highest; 51 lowest

Cost of Living - average statewide (rank) 21
Per Capita Income (rank / $) .... 17 / 40,852
Median Household Income (rank / $) .... 11 / 58,380
Median House Value (rank / $).........................15 / 239,700
Median Property Tax on Homes (rank) 40
Fuel - avg per gal $, Mar 2010 (diesel / gas) .....2.92 / 2.66
Fuel Taxes - per gallon $ (diesel / gas)...........0.464 / 0.414
Cigarette Tax - pack of 20 ($) 2.61
Tax Burden - average all taxes (rank) 25

STATE & LOCAL REVENUE SOURCES

Rank: 1 highest; 51 lowest
Rank and % of total revenue from:

Tax Revenue (see "Details" listed below) ....31 / 39.65
Charges & Misc. Revenue...02 / 29.38
Federal Government ....40 / 13.70
Utility Revenue ....22 / 04.14
Insurance Trust Revenue..41 / 13.13

Tax Revenue Details (rank / %)
Property Tax...48 / 15.55
Sales & Gross Receipts ....49 / 12.78
Individual Income Tax...13 / 29.35
Corporate Income Tax...05 / 08.26
Motor Vehicle License...39 / 00.95
Other Taxes ....02 / 33.13

POPULATION

Rank: 1 highest; 51 lowest

State Population (rank / count) ....45 / 885,122
Population Per Square Mile (rank / count) ....08 / 356

VOTING

Registration Requirements: In-person registration deadline is the fourth Saturday before election.

Address Requirements: Physical/street address required.

Register by Mail: Yes.

Absentee Voting: Yes, excuse required.

Web Site: www.elections.delaware.gov/

RESOURCES

Delaware State Government
Phone: 800-273-9500
Web Site: www.delaware.gov

Delaware Division of Revenue
Phone: 302-577-8200
Web Site: www.revenue.delaware.gov

Delaware Division of Motor Vehicles
Phone: 302-434-3200
Web Site: www.dmv.de.gov

Delaware Office of Tourism
Phone: 866-284-7483
Web Site: www.visitdelaware.com

District of Columbia

WEATHER

	Washington		
	🌡	💧	❄
Jan	43/28	2.8	5.3
Feb	46/30	2.6	5.3
Mar	55/37	3.4	2.1
Apr	67/46	2.8	0
May	76/56	3.9	0
Jun	84/65	3.3	0
Jul	88/70	4	0
Aug	86/69	4.1	0
Sep	80/62	3.3	0
Oct	69/50	3	0
Nov	58/40	3	0.8
Dec	47/32	3.1	3.1
🌡	Average monthly high and low temperatures in degrees Fahrenheit.		
💧	Average monthly precipitation totals in inches.		
❄	Average monthly snowfall totals in inches.		

STATE AND LOCAL TAXES

State Sales Tax (%) 6.00
Exempt: food and prescription drugs.

Local Sales Taxes (up to an additional %) .... None
Inheritance Tax .... No
Estate Tax..Yes
Limited.

PERSONAL INCOME TAXES

State Income Tax (%) .... 4 - 8.5
3 income brackets - Lowest $10,000; Highest $40,000.

Personal Exemption $ (single / joint) ....1,675 / 1,675
Standard Deduction $ (single / joint)............4,000 / 4,000
Federal Income Tax Paid - Deduction Allowed .... None
Social Security Income - Tax Exempt...............................Yes
Retired Military Pay - Tax Exempt .... Limits
State & Local Government Pensions - Tax Exempt .. Limits
Federal Civil Service Pensions - Tax Exempt .... Limits

Railroad Retirement - Tax Exempt ....Yes
Private Pension - Tax Exempt .... No
Note: Limits include a maximum combined exemption of $3,000 (for taxpayers 62 or older) from all retirement income sources other than Social Security and Railroad Retirement.

VEHICLES

Registration Fees .... 1 Year
Passenger Class A vehicles, rate based on weight:
3,499 lbs or less, $72.
3,500 - 4,999 lbs, $115.
5,000 lbs or more, $155.

Trailer Class C vehicle, rate based on weight:
1,499 lbs or less, $50.
1,500 - 3,499 lbs, $125.
3,500 - 4,999 lbs, $250.
5,000 - 6,999 lbs, $400.
7,000 - 10,999 lbs, $500.
11,000 - 11,999 lbs, $550.
For each additional 1,000 lbs over 11,000 lbs, $50.

Annual Vehicle Tax .... No
No property tax on vehicles.

State Emissions Test Required ....Yes
Every two years.
Web Site: www.dmv.dc.gov/serv/inspections.shtm

Vehicle Safety Inspection Required ....Yes
Every two years.

Mandatory Minimum Liability Insurance 25/50/10
Uninsured Motorist coverage is also required.

COST OF LIVING INDICATORS

Rank: 1 highest; 51 lowest

Cost of Living - average statewide (rank) 02
Per Capita Income (rank / $) ....01 / 64,991
Median Household Income (rank / $) .... 10 / 58,553
Median House Value (rank / $).........................03 / 453,900
Median Property Tax on Homes (rank) 19
Fuel - avg per gal $, Mar 2010 (diesel / gas).....3.05 / 2.81
Fuel Taxes - per gallon $ (diesel / gas)...........0.479 / 0.419
Cigarette Tax - pack of 20 ($) 3.51
Tax Burden - average all taxes (rank) 08

STATE & LOCAL REVENUE SOURCES

Rank: 1 highest; 51 lowest
Rank and % of total revenue from:

Tax Revenue (see "Details" listed below) ....12 / 45.59
Charges & Misc. Revenue..50 / 13.66
Federal Government ....03 / 26.33
Utility Revenue ....07 / 07.14
Insurance Trust Revenue..51 / 07.28

Tax Revenue Details (rank / %)

Property Tax...24 / 29.20
Sales & Gross Receipts ....41 / 25.62
Individual Income Tax..20 / 25.29
Corporate Income Tax...07 / 08.03
Motor Vehicle License...44 / 00.50
Other Taxes ....09 / 11.36

POPULATION

Rank: 1 highest; 51 lowest

State Population (rank / count) ....50 / 599,657
Population Per Square Mile (rank / count) ....01 / 8,818

VOTING

Registration Requirements: In-person registration deadline is 30 days before election.

Address Requirements: Physical/street address required.

Register by Mail: Yes, registration deadline is 30 days before election.

Absentee Voting: Yes, excuse required.

Web Site: www.dcboee.org

RESOURCES

District of Columbia Government
Phone: 202-727-2277
Web Site: www.dc.gov

Washington DC Office of Tax and Revenue
Phone: 202-727-4829
Web Site: www.otr.cfo.dc.gov

Washington DC Department of Motor Vehicles
Phone: 202-737-4404
Web Site: www.dmv.dc.gov

Washington DC Office of Tourism
Phone: 800-422-8644
Web Site: www.washington.org

Florida

WEATHER

	Jacksonville			Orlando		
	🌡	💧	❄	🌡	💧	❄
Jan	65/43	3.3	N/A	72/50	2.1	N/A
Feb	68/45	3.5	N/A	73/51	3.1	N/A
Mar	74/51	3.9	N/A	77/55	3.5	N/A
Apr	80/56	3	N/A	83/61	2.6	N/A
May	86/64	3.6	N/A	88/67	3	N/A
Jun	90/70	5.6	N/A	91/71	6.5	N/A
Jul	92/73	6.5	N/A	92/73	8.1	N/A
Aug	91/73	7.3	N/A	92/73	7.2	N/A
Sep	87/70	7.7	N/A	89/72	6.8	N/A
Oct	80/61	4.1	N/A	84/66	3.9	N/A
Nov	73/51	2	N/A	77/56	1.7	N/A
Dec	67/44	2.5	N/A	73/51	2.1	N/A
🌡	Average monthly high and low temperatures in degrees Fahrenheit.					
💧	Average monthly precipitation totals in inches.					
❄	Average monthly snowfall totals in inches.					

STATE AND LOCAL TAXES

State Sales Tax (%) 6.00
Exempt: food and prescription drugs.

Local Sales Taxes (up to an additional %) 3.50
Inheritance Tax .... No
Estate Tax...Yes
Limited.

PERSONAL INCOME TAXES

State Income Tax (%) .... None
Personal Exemption $ (single / joint) .... n/a
Standard Deduction $ (single / joint)............................... n/a
Federal Income Tax Paid - Deduction Allowed .... n/a
Social Security Income - Tax Exempt................................. n/a
Retired Military Pay - Tax Exempt .... n/a
State & Local Government Pensions - Tax Exempt .... n/a
Federal Civil Service Pensions - Tax Exempt .... n/a

Railroad Retirement - Tax Exempt .... n/a
Private Pension - Tax Exempt .... n/a

VEHICLES

Registration Fees .... 1 Year
*For automobiles, trucks, campers, and motor homes. Fee
varies with type of vehicle, length, and weight, $13.50 -
$47.50.*

*Initial registration fee, $225. This is charged in addition
to the basic fees when applicant does not have a Florida
registration to transfer.*

*If you purchased a vehicle less than six months before
registering it in Florida you are required to pay sales or
use tax and local discretionary sales surtax. If you owe
6% to Florida and you paid 4% in your previous state you
will only owe the difference. If you bought the vehicle
more than 6 months ago no tax is due.*

Annual Vehicle Tax .... No
No property tax on vehicles.

State Emissions Test Required .... No
Vehicle Safety Inspection Required .... No
Mandatory Minimum Liability Insurance 10/20/10
Personal Injury Protection is also required.

COST OF LIVING INDICATORS

Rank: 1 highest; 51 lowest

Cost of Living - average statewide (rank) 22
Per Capita Income (rank / $) .... 22 / 39,070
Median Household Income (rank / $) .... 34 / 47,802
Median House Value (rank / $) .... 19 / 226,300
Median Property Tax on Homes (rank) 22
Fuel - avg per gal $, Mar 2010 (diesel / gas) .....2.90 / 2.76
Fuel Taxes - per gallon $ (diesel / gas) ....0.426 / 0.421
County and local taxes can add up to 12 cents.
Cigarette Tax - pack of 20 ($) 2.35
Tax Burden - average all taxes (rank) 48

STATE & LOCAL REVENUE SOURCES

Rank: 1 highest; 51 lowest
Rank and % of total revenue from:

Tax Revenue (see "Details" listed below) ....22 / 42.21
Charges & Misc. Revenue...17 / 21.85
Federal Government ....43 / 13.29
Utility Revenue ....13 / 04.87
Insurance Trust Revenue...21 / 17.78

Tax Revenue Details (rank / %)
Property Tax...10 / 36.78
Sales & Gross Receipts ....08 / 48.91
Individual Income Tax..44 / 0
Corporate Income Tax...32 / 03.35
Motor Vehicle License...24 / 01.63
Other Taxes ....14 / 9.33

POPULATION

Rank: 1 highest; 51 lowest

State Population (rank / count) ....04 / 18,537,969
Population Per Square Mile (rank / count) ....09 / 282

VOTING

Registration Requirements: In-person registration
deadline is 30 days before election.

Address Requirements: Physical/street address required.

Register by Mail: Yes, registration deadline is 29 days
before election.

Absentee Voting: Yes, no excuse is required.

Web Site: http://election.dos.state.fl.us/

RESOURCES

Florida State Government
Phone: 850-488-1234
Web Site: www.myflorida.com

Florida Department of Revenue
Phone: 800-352-3671
Web Site: www.myflorida.com/dor

Florida Dept. of Highway Safety and Motor Vehicles
Phone: 850-617-2000
Web Site: www.flhsmv.gov

Florida Office of Tourism
Phone: 888-735-2872
Web Site: www.visitflorida.com

Georgia

WEATHER

	Atlanta			Savannah		
	🌡	💧	❄	🌡	💧	❄
Jan	52/33	4.7	0.9	60/38	3.5	N/A
Feb	56/36	4.6	0.5	64/41	3.1	N/A
Mar	64/43	5.6	0.4	70/48	3.9	N/A
Apr	73/51	4.1	0	78/54	3.2	N/A
May	80/59	4	0	84/62	4.2	N/A
Jun	86/67	3.7	0	89/69	5.6	N/A
Jul	89/70	5.3	0	92/72	6.8	N/A
Aug	88/69	3.7	0	90/72	7.2	N/A
Sep	82/64	3.6	0	86/68	5	N/A
Oct	73/53	3	0	78/57	2.9	N/A
Nov	63/42	4	0	70/47	2.2	N/A
Dec	54/36	4.1	0.2	62/40	2.7	N/A
🌡	Average monthly high and low temperatures in degrees Fahrenheit.					
💧	Average monthly precipitation totals in inches.					
❄	Average monthly snowfall totals in inches.					

STATE AND LOCAL TAXES

State Sales Tax (%) 4.00
Exempt: food and prescription drugs.

Local Sales Taxes (up to an additional %) 3.00
Food is subject to local taxes.

Inheritance Tax .... No
Estate Tax ....Yes
Limited.

PERSONAL INCOME TAXES

State Income Tax (%) ....1 - 6
6 income brackets - Lowest $750; Highest $7,000. ($1,000 to $10,000 for joint filers.)

Personal Exemption $ (single / joint) ....2,700 / 5,400
Standard Deduction $ (single / joint) ....2,300 / 3,000
Additional $1,300 if age 65 or over.

Federal Income Tax Paid - Deduction Allowed .... None
Social Security Income - Tax Exempt ....Yes

Retired Military Pay - Tax Exempt ....Limits
State & Local Government Pensions - Tax Exempt .. Limits
Federal Civil Service Pensions - Tax Exempt ....Limits
Railroad Retirement - Tax Exempt ....Yes
Private Pension - Tax Exempt ....Limits

Note: Limits include a maximum combined exemption of $35,000 (for taxpayers 62 or older) from all retirement income sources other than Social Security and Railroad Retirement.

VEHICLES

Registration Fees .... 1 Year
Passenger vehicle and trucks 14,000 lbs or less, $20.
Trucks 14,001 - 30,000 lbs, $45.
Trucks 30,001 - 36,000 lbs, $70.

Annual Vehicle Tax ....Yes
Annual property tax on vehicles. There is a rate calculator at the Department of Revenue web site. In addition to the vehicle information you will need to know the county and tax district.

State Emissions Test Required ....Yes
Annual. Vehicles up to 8,500 lbs in 13 metro-Atlanta counties only. RVs, motor homes, and diesel powered vehicles are exempt. Web Site: www.cleanairforce.com

Vehicle Safety Inspection Required .... No
Mandatory Minimum Liability Insurance 25/50/25

COST OF LIVING INDICATORS

Rank: 1 highest; 51 lowest

Cost of Living - average statewide (rank) 45
Per Capita Income (rank / $) ....41 / 33,975
Median Household Income (rank / $) ....24 / 50,834
Median House Value (rank / $) ....29 / 163,500
Median Property Tax on Homes (rank) 35
Fuel - avg per gal $, Mar 2010 (diesel / gas) .....2.81 / 2.65
Fuel Taxes - per gallon $ (diesel / gas) ....0.422 / 0.330
Plus local sales taxes.

Cigarette Tax - pack of 20 ($) 1.38
Tax Burden - average all taxes (rank) 17

STATE & LOCAL REVENUE SOURCES

Rank: 1 highest; 51 lowest
Rank and % of total revenue from:

Tax Revenue (see "Details" listed below) ....16 / 43.60
Charges & Misc. Revenue ....26 / 20.25
Federal Government ....18 / 18.14

Utility Revenue...09 / 05.67
Insurance Trust Revenue.................................44 / 12.34

Tax Revenue Details (rank / %)

Property Tax..27 / 28.71
Sales & Gross Receipts ....15 / 38.53
Individual Income Tax.......................................17 / 26.54
Corporate Income Tax.......................................35 / 03.07
Motor Vehicle License.......................................41 / 00.87
Other Taxes ....51 / 02.28

POPULATION

Rank: 1 highest; 51 lowest

State Population (rank / count) ....09 / 9,829,211
Population Per Square Mile (rank / count) ....17 / 165

VOTING

Registration Requirements: In-person registration deadline is the fifth Monday before election.

Address Requirements: Physical/street address required.

Register by Mail: Yes, deadline is the fifth Monday before election.

Absentee Voting: Yes, no excuse is required.

Web Site: www.sos.ga.gov/elections/

RESOURCES

Georgia State Government
Phone: 866-351-0001
Web Site: www.georgia.gov

Georgia Department of Revenue
Phone: 404-417-4477
Web Site: www.etax.dor.ga.gov

Georgia Motor Vehicle Division
Phone: 404-968-3800
Web Site: http://motor.etax.dor.ga.gov

Georgia Department of Driver Services (Drivers License)
Phone: 678-413-8400
Web Site: www.dds.ga.gov

Georgia Office of Tourism
Phone: 800-847-4842
Web Site: www.georgia.org/travel

Hawaii

WEATHER

	Honolulu		
	🌡	💧	❄
Jan	80/66	3.4	N/A
Feb	80/66	2.6	N/A
Mar	81/67	2.8	N/A
Apr	82/69	1.3	N/A
May	84/70	1	N/A
Jun	86/72	0.4	N/A
Jul	87/73	0.6	N/A
Aug	88/74	0.6	N/A
Sep	88/74	0.7	N/A
Oct	86/72	2	N/A
Nov	84/70	2.6	N/A
Dec	81/67	3.5	N/A
🌡	Average monthly high and low temperatures in degrees Fahrenheit.		
💧	Average monthly precipitation totals in inches.		
❄	Average monthly snowfall totals in inches.		

STATE AND LOCAL TAXES

State Sales Tax (%)..See note
Hawaii has a gross receipts tax of 0.15% to 4%, depending on the business activity. Common consumer transactions are at the 4% level. Exempt: prescription drugs.

Local Sales Taxes (up to an additional %) 0.5
Inheritance Tax .... No
Estate Tax...Yes
Limited to federal estate tax collection.

PERSONAL INCOME TAXES

State Income Tax (%) ....1.4 - 11
12 income brackets - Lowest $2,400; Highest $200,000.

Personal Exemption $ (single / joint) ....1,040 / 2,080
Standard Deduction $ (single / joint)...........2,200 / 4,400

Federal Income Tax Paid - Deduction Allowed .... None

Social Security Income - Tax Exempt ....Yes

Retired Military Pay - Tax Exempt ....Yes

State & Local Government Pensions - Tax Exempt ....Yes

Federal Civil Service Pensions - Tax Exempt ....Yes

Railroad Retirement - Tax Exempt ....Yes

Private Pension - Tax Exempt ....Yes

VEHICLES

Registration Fees .... 1 Year

Hawaii has different rules and fees for each county government. Base fees are $30 plus. Additional fees are based on vehicle weight and usage.

The annual state tax rates "per pound" are as follows:
Up to 4,000 lbs, 0.75 cents.
4,000 to 7,000 lbs, 1 cent.
7,000 to 10,000 lbs, 1.25 cents.
For vehicles weighing over 10,000 lbs, $150 flat fee.

City and county taxes can add an additional 1 to 2 cents per pound.

Annual Vehicle Tax ....Yes

Fees are included in vehicle registration. No property tax on vehicles.

State Emissions Test Required .... No

Vehicle Safety Inspection Required ....Yes

Annual.

Mandatory Minimum Liability Insurance 20/40/10

Personal Injury Protection is also required.

COST OF LIVING INDICATORS

Rank: 1 highest; 51 lowest

Cost of Living - average statewide (rank) 01

Per Capita Income (rank / $) .... 18 / 40,490

Median Household Income (rank / $) ....05 / 66,701

Median House Value (rank / $).........................01 / 548,700

Median Property Tax on Homes (rank) 32

Fuel - avg per gal $, Mar 2010 (diesel / gas).....3.93 / 3.46

Fuel Taxes - per gallon $ (diesel / gas)...........0.415 / 0.355

Sales tax plus county taxes can add up to 30 cents.

Cigarette Tax - pack of 20 ($) 3.61

Tax Burden - average all taxes (rank) 05

STATE & LOCAL REVENUE SOURCES

Rank: 1 highest; 51 lowest
Rank and % of total revenue from:

Tax Revenue (see "Details" listed below) ....04 / 48.44

Charges & Misc. Revenue..38 / 17.98

Federal Government ....24 / 16.50

Utility Revenue ....43 / 01.56

Insurance Trust Revenue...32 / 15.52

Tax Revenue Details (rank / %)

Property Tax..45 / 17.32

Sales & Gross Receipts ....07 / 51.79

Individual Income Tax...25 / 23.76

Corporate Income Tax...45 / 01.54

Motor Vehicle License ....05 / 03.30

Other Taxes ....50 / 02.29

POPULATION

Rank: 1 highest; 51 lowest

State Population (rank / count) .... 42 / 1,295,178

Population Per Square Mile (rank / count) .... 21 / 118

VOTING

Registration Requirements: In-person registration deadline is 30 days before election.

Address Requirements: Physical/street address required.

Register by Mail: Yes, registration deadline is 30 days before election.

Absentee Voting: Yes, no excuse is required.

Web Site: http://hawaii.gov/elections

RESOURCES

Hawaii State Government
Phone: 866-462-3468
Web Site: www.ehawaii.gov

Hawaii Department of Taxation
Phone: 808-587-4242
Web Site: www.hawaii.gov/tax

Hawaii Department of Motor Vehicles
Hawaii does not have a statewide Department of Motor Vehicles. Vehicle registration is managed by each county government.
Phone: 808-587-2160

City & County of Honolulu
Web Site: www.honolulu.gov/csd/vehicle/mvehicle.htm

County of Maui
Web Site: hi-mauicounty.civicplus.com/index?NID=554

County of Hawaii
Web Site: www.co.hawaii.hi.us/info/mvr/fees/htm

County of Kauai
Web Site: www.kauai.gov

Hawaii Office of Tourism
Phone: 800-464-2924
Web Site: www.gohawaii.com

Idaho

WEATHER

	Boise			Coeur d'Alene		
	🌡	💧	❄	🌡	💧	❄
Jan	36/22	1.4	6.8	29/16	2.1	29.9
Feb	44/27	1.1	3.6	37/22	1.8	15.1
Mar	53/31	1.2	1.7	43/27	1.7	9.8
Apr	62/37	1.2	0.6	57/33	0.9	0.1
May	71/44	1.2	0.1	65/41	1.1	0.2
Jun	80/52	0.9	0	72/47	1.8	0
Jul	90/58	0.3	0	81/51	0.3	0
Aug	88/57	0.3	0	80/51	0.7	0
Sep	78/48	0.6	0	73/44	0.7	0
Oct	65/39	0.7	0.1	57/36	2.7	0.3
Nov	48/30	1.4	2.2	43/30	1.8	3.1
Dec	38/23	1.4	5.8	33/23	2.2	26.7

🌡	Average monthly high and low temperatures in degrees Fahrenheit.
💧	Average monthly precipitation totals in inches.
❄	Average monthly snowfall totals in inches.

STATE AND LOCAL TAXES

State Sales Tax (%) 6.00
  Exempt: prescription drugs.

Local Sales Taxes (up to an additional %) 3.00
Inheritance Tax .... No
Estate Tax... No

PERSONAL INCOME TAXES

State Income Tax (%) ....1.6 - 7.8
  8 income brackets - Lowest $1,272; Highest $25,441.

Personal Exemption $ (single / joint) ....3,200 / 6,400
Standard Deduction $ (single / joint).........6,250 / 11,000
Federal Income Tax Paid - Deduction Allowed .... None
Social Security Income - Tax Exempt................................Yes
Retired Military Pay - Tax Exempt ....Limits
State & Local Government Pensions - Tax Exempt .. Limits
  Limited to some public safety officer's benefits.

Federal Civil Service Pensions - Tax Exempt .... Limits
Railroad Retirement - Tax Exempt ....Yes
Private Pension - Tax Exempt .... No

Note: Limits include a maximum combined exemption of $27,876 (for taxpayers 65 or older) from all retirement income including Social Security and Railroad Retirement.

VEHICLES

Registration Fees .... 1 Year
The total cost varies with type or weight of vehicle, age, and county of residence. Basic fees for passenger vehicles and pickup trucks having a maximum gross weight 8,000 lbs or less, $24 - $48.

In addition to the basic fee, motor homes require a recreational vehicle stickers which cost $8.50 for the first $1,000 of market value, plus $5.00 for each additional $1,000 of market value. To determine the market value, multiply the overall value of your motor home by the following pre-determined chassis valuation factors.
Class A Motor Home, 60%
Class A front engine diesel, 45%
Class A rear engine diesel, 58%
Class C Mini Motor Home, 50%
Class B Van Conversion, 25%

The result is the RV value used to determine RV sticker fees. Example: For a 5-year old Class C with a value of $30,000. (Value $30,000 x 50% = RV Valuation of $15,000.) $36.00 for basic registration fee, for a vehicle three to six years old. $8.50 for the first $1,000 of RV Valuation. $70.00 from the additional value above the first $1,000 ($5.00 x 14). The total basic registration fee for the above motor home is $114.50. Some miscellaneous and county administrative fees may be additional.

Other recreational vehicles such as camp trailers, tent trailers, and fifth wheels are required to pay a $4 registration fee plus an recreational vehicle fee. RV fees for these types of vehicles are based on 100% of market value. The fees are $8.50 for the first $1,000 of market value, plus $5 for each additional $1,000 of market value.

Annual Vehicle Tax ....Yes
Fees are included in vehicle registration. No property tax on vehicles.

State Emissions Test Required ....Yes
In Ada County only. Motorhomes and vehicles under 1,500 lbs GVWR are exempt.
Web Site: www.emissiontest.org

Vehicle Safety Inspection Required .... No
Mandatory Minimum Liability Insurance 25/50/15

COST OF LIVING INDICATORS
Rank: 1 highest; 51 lowest

Cost of Living - average statewide (rank) 39
Per Capita Income (rank / $) ....44 / 32,133
Median Household Income (rank / $) ....35 / 47,561
Median House Value (rank / $).........................25 / 174,800
Median Property Tax on Homes (rank) 37
Fuel - avg per gal $, Mar 2010 (diesel / gas).....2.93 / 2.74
Fuel Taxes - per gallon $ (diesel / gas)...........0.494 / 0.434
Cigarette Tax - pack of 20 ($) 1.58
Tax Burden - average all taxes (rank) 14

STATE & LOCAL REVENUE SOURCES
Rank: 1 highest; 51 lowest
Rank and % of total revenue from:

Tax Revenue (see "Details" listed below) ....35 / 38.58
Charges & Misc. Revenue.......................................13 / 22.72
Federal Government ....28 / 16.02
Utility Revenue ....40 / 01.77
Insurance Trust Revenue..09 / 20.91

Tax Revenue Details (rank / %)

Property Tax...39 / 23.40
Sales & Gross Receipts ....21 / 35.73
Individual Income Tax...11 / 29.53
Corporate Income Tax...27 / 03.95
Motor Vehicle License ....06 / 02.75
Other Taxes ....32 / 04.64

POPULATION
Rank: 1 highest; 51 lowest

State Population (rank / count) ....39 / 1,545,801
Population Per Square Mile (rank / count) .... 45 / 18

VOTING

Registration Requirements: In-person registration deadline is the day of election.

Address Requirements: Physical/street address required.

Register by Mail: Yes, registration deadline is 25 days before election.

Absentee Voting: Yes, no excuse is required.

Web Site: www.idahovotes.gov/

RESOURCES

Idaho State Government
Phone: 208-334-2411
Web Site: www.idaho.gov

Idaho State Tax Commission
Phone: 208-334-8735
Web Site: www.tax.idaho.gov

Idaho Division of Motor Vehicles
Phone: 800-847-4843
Web Site: www.itd.idaho.gov/dmv

Idaho Office of Tourism
Phone: 800-972-7660
Web Site: www.visitidaho.org

Illinois

WEATHER

	Chicago			Springfield		
	🌡	💧	❄	🌡	💧	❄
Jan	29/13	1.7	10.7	35/19	1.8	5.8
Feb	34/18	1.4	8.1	38/22	1.7	6.4
Mar	45/28	2.7	7	50/32	3.1	4.1
Apr	58/39	3.6	1.7	63/43	3.6	0.7
May	70/48	3.2	0.1	74/53	3.8	0
Jun	80/57	3.8	0	84/63	3.9	0
Jul	84/63	3.6	0	88/67	3.3	0
Aug	82/62	4.1	0	85/65	3.1	0
Sep	75/54	3.5	0	79/57	3.3	0
Oct	63/42	2.6	0.4	67/46	2.6	0
Nov	48/31	2.9	1.9	51/34	2.4	1.7
Dec	35/20	2.2	8.3	38/24	2.1	4.9
🌡	Average monthly high and low temperatures in degrees Fahrenheit.					
💧	Average monthly precipitation totals in inches.					
❄	Average monthly snowfall totals in inches.					

STATE AND LOCAL TAXES

State Sales Tax (%) 6.25
    1% tax on qualifying food and prescription drugs.

Local Sales Taxes (up to an additional %) 5.25
Inheritance Tax .... No
Estate Tax...Yes
    Limited to federal estate tax collection.

PERSONAL INCOME TAXES

State Income Tax (%) 3
    Flat rate, no income brackets.

Personal Exemption $ (single / joint) ....2,000 / 4,000
Standard Deduction $ (single / joint)............................ None
Federal Income Tax Paid - Deduction Allowed .... None
Social Security Income - Tax Exempt ....Yes
Retired Military Pay - Tax Exempt ....Yes
State & Local Government Pensions - Tax Exempt ....Yes
Federal Civil Service Pensions - Tax Exempt ....Yes

Railroad Retirement - Tax Exempt .... Yes
Private Pension - Tax Exempt .... Limits
  Exempt for qualified plans.

VEHICLES

Registration Fees .... 1 Year
  Passenger vehicles and trucks up to 8,000 lbs, $99.
  Recreational trailer, fee is based on weight:
  3,000 lbs or less, $18.
  3,001 - 8,000 lbs, $30.
  8,001 - 10,000 lbs, $38.
  10,001 lbs and over, $50.

  Recreational vehicle, fee is based on weight:
  8,000 lbs or less, $78.
  8,0001 - 10,000 lbs, $90.
  10,000 lbs and over, $102.

Annual Vehicle Tax .... No
  No property tax on vehicles.

State Emissions Test Required .... Yes
  Every two years. Vehicles registered in specific ZIP codes in the Northeastern Illinois and Metro-East St. Louis areas are subject to testing. Diesel-powered vehicles are exempt. Web Site: www.epa.state.il.us/air/vim

Vehicle Safety Inspection Required .... No
Mandatory Minimum Liability Insurance 20/40/15
  Uninsured Motorist coverage is also required.

COST OF LIVING INDICATORS
  Rank: 1 highest; 51 lowest

Cost of Living - average statewide (rank) 32
Per Capita Income (rank / $) .... 13 / 42,397
Median Household Income (rank / $) .... 17 / 56,230
Median House Value (rank / $) .... 22 / 208,000
Median Property Tax on Homes (rank) 07
Fuel - avg per gal $, Mar 2010 (diesel / gas) .....2.96 / 2.76
Fuel Taxes - per gallon $ (diesel / gas)............0.459 / 0.374
  State and local sales taxes can add 20 cents.

Cigarette Tax - pack of 20 ($) 1.99
  Additional $2 tax in Cook County plus city taxes of 68 cents in Chicago, 50 in Evanston, 16 in Cicero, and 5 cents in Rosemont.

Tax Burden - average all taxes (rank) 31

STATE & LOCAL REVENUE SOURCES
  Rank: 1 highest; 51 lowest
  Rank and % of total revenue from:

Tax Revenue (see "Details" listed below) ....06 / 46.10

Charges & Misc. Revenue...48 / 16.05
Federal Government ....39 / 14.15
Utility Revenue ....30 / 02.73
Insurance Trust Revenue...08 / 20.97

  Tax Revenue Details (rank / %)

Property Tax..08 / 37.15
Sales & Gross Receipts ....27 / 33.76
Individual Income Tax...37 / 17.08
Corporate Income Tax...14 / 05.33
Motor Vehicle License...11 / 02.50
Other Taxes ....36 / 04.18

POPULATION
  Rank: 1 highest; 51 lowest

State Population (rank / count) ....05 / 12,910,409
Population Per Square Mile (rank / count) ....13 / 223

VOTING

Registration Requirements: In-person registration deadline is 28 days before election.

Address Requirements: Physical/street address required.

Register by Mail: Yes, registration deadline is 28 days before election.

Absentee Voting: Yes, excuse required.

Web Site: www.elections.state.il.us/

RESOURCES

Illinois State Government
Phone: 217-782-0244
Web Site: www.illinois.gov

Illinois Department of Revenue
Phone: 800-732-8866
Web Site: www.revenue.state.il.us

Illinois Driver Services Department
Phone: 217-782-7132
Web Site: www.cyberdriveillinois.com

Illinois Office of Tourism
Phone: 800-226-6632
Web Site: www.enjoyillinois.com

Indiana

WEATHER

	Indianapolis			South Bend		
	🌡	💧	❄	🌡	💧	❄
Jan	35/19	2.7	6.1	31/17	2.4	18.9
Feb	39/22	2.4	5.8	34/19	2	14.9
Mar	50/31	3.6	3.4	45/28	2.9	9.1
Apr	63/42	3.7	0.5	59/38	3.7	2
May	73/52	3.9	0	70/48	3.1	0
Jun	82/61	3.9	0	80/58	4	0
Jul	85/65	4.4	0	83/63	3.8	0
Aug	84/63	3.4	0	81/61	3.7	0
Sep	77/55	2.9	0	74/54	3.5	0
Oct	66/44	2.7	0.2	63/43	3.3	0.7
Nov	51/33	3.5	1.8	48/33	3.2	8
Dec	39/24	3.1	4.9	36/22	3	17.7
🌡	Average monthly high and low temperatures in degrees Fahrenheit.					
💧	Average monthly precipitation totals in inches.					
❄	Average monthly snowfall totals in inches.					

STATE AND LOCAL TAXES

State Sales Tax (%) 7.00
Exempt: food and prescription drugs.

Local Sales Taxes (up to an additional %) .... None

Inheritance Tax ....Yes
Ranges from 1% to 10% of fair market value.

Estate Tax..Yes
Limited.

PERSONAL INCOME TAXES

State Income Tax (%) 3.4
Flat rate, no income brackets. City and/or county income taxes not included.

Personal Exemption $ (single / joint) ....1,000 / 2,000
Additional $500 if age 65 or over.

Standard Deduction $ (single / joint)........................... None
Federal Income Tax Paid - Deduction Allowed .... None
Social Security Income - Tax Exempt..................................Yes

Retired Military Pay - Tax Exempt ....Limits
Up to $5,000 (if 60 or older) less Social Security benefits.

State & Local Government Pensions - Tax Exempt .... No
Federal Civil Service Pensions - Tax Exempt ....Limits
Up to $2,000 (if 60 or older) less Social Security benefits.

Railroad Retirement - Tax Exempt ....Yes
Private Pension - Tax Exempt .... No

VEHICLES

Registration Fees .... 1 Year
Passenger cars, $21.05.

Truck fees are based on weight:
7,000 lbs or less, $30.05.
7,001 - 16,000, $50.05 - $144.75.
16,001 - 30,000, $184.75 - $304.75
30,001 - 66,001 or more, $422.75 - $965.75.

Recreational vehicle, $29.75

Annual Vehicle Tax ....Yes
An annual excise tax is charged in lieu of property tax. Some counties also have a surtax or wheel tax. The excise tax varies with age, type, and value (manufacture's original retail price) of vehicle. Fees can range from $12 to over $500 for passenger cars and more than $2,000 for motor homes.

Examples: For a 3 year old passenger vehicle with an original value of $15,000 the excise tax would be $156. For a 3 year old RV with an original value of $70,000 the tax is $782.

A chart showing the Excise Tax Fees for passenger cars and recreational vehicles is available at the Bureau of Motor Vehicles web site. Click on "Fees" then under Vehicle Taxes click on "Learn more about excise tax rates".

Some counties charge a flat rate for the "surtax or wheel tax" anywhere from $10 to $25. Other counties charge a "%" fee. From the Bureau of Motor Vehicles web site click on "Fees" the under Vehicle Taxes click on "Learn more about surtax or wheel tax rates" for a list of counties and the rate they charge.

State Emissions Test Required ....Yes
Every two years. Lake and Porter counties only. Diesel powered and recreational vehicles are exempt.
Web Site: www.cleanaircarcheck.com

Vehicle Safety Inspection Required .... No
Mandatory Minimum Liability Insurance 25/50/10

COST OF LIVING INDICATORS

Rank: 1 highest; 51 lowest

Cost of Living - average statewide (rank) 40
Per Capita Income (rank / $) .... 40 / 34,103
Median Household Income (rank / $) .... 33 / 48,010
Median House Value (rank / $) .... 39 / 122,800
Median Property Tax on Homes (rank) 38
Fuel - avg per gal $, Mar 2010 (diesel / gas) .....2.88 / 2.62
Fuel Taxes - per gallon $ (diesel / gas) ....0.524 / 0.374
State sales tax adds about 15 cents.

Cigarette Tax - pack of 20 ($) 2.01
Tax Burden - average all taxes (rank) 29

STATE & LOCAL REVENUE SOURCES

Rank: 1 highest; 51 lowest
Rank and % of total revenue from:

Tax Revenue (see "Details" listed below) ....19 / 43.03
Charges & Misc. Revenue ....06 / 25.40
Federal Government ....23 / 16.69
Utility Revenue ....18 / 04.32
Insurance Trust Revenue ....47 / 10.56

Tax Revenue Details (rank / %)

Property Tax ....25 / 29.12
Sales & Gross Receipts ....19 / 37.17
Individual Income Tax ....22 / 24.72
Corporate Income Tax ....20 / 04.68
Motor Vehicle License ....35 / 01.19
Other Taxes ....46 / 03.12

POPULATION

Rank: 1 highest; 51 lowest

State Population (rank / count) .... 16 / 6,423,113
Population Per Square Mile (rank / count) ....15 / 176

VOTING

Registration Requirements: In-person registration deadline is 29 days before election.

Address Requirements: Physical/street address required.

Register by Mail: Yes, registration deadline is 29 days before election.

Absentee Voting: Yes, excuse required.

Web Site: www.in.gov/sos/elections/

RESOURCES

Indiana State Government
Phone: 800-457-8283
Web Site: www.in.gov

Indiana Department of Revenue
Phone: 317-233-4018
Web Site: www.in.gov/dor

Indiana Bureau of Motor Vehicles
Phone: 317-233-6000
Web Site: www.state.in.us/bmv

Indiana Office of Tourism
Phone: 888-365-6946
Web Site: www.visitindiana.com

Iowa

WEATHER

	Cedar Rapids			Des Moines		
	🌡	💧	❄	🌡	💧	❄
Jan	30/10	1.6	6.6	29/11	1.1	8.1
Feb	36/16	2.2	6.1	34/16	1.2	7.2
Mar	42/23	3.2	11.2	46/27	2.3	6.2
Apr	60/36	3.3	0.4	61/40	3.3	1.9
May	71/48	3.6	0	72/51	4	0
Jun	82/60	5	0	82/61	4.3	0
Jul	86/63	4.2	0	86/66	3.7	0
Aug	83/60	3.1	0	84/64	4	0
Sep	77/50	1.9	0	76/54	3.1	0
Oct	66/39	1.7	0	65/43	2.3	0.2
Nov	48/27	2.1	0.7	47/29	1.8	3
Dec	34/16	1.6	7.4	34/17	1.3	6.6

🌡	Average monthly high and low temperatures in degrees Fahrenheit.
💧	Average monthly precipitation totals in inches.
❄	Average monthly snowfall totals in inches.

STATE AND LOCAL TAXES

State Sales Tax (%) 6.00
  Exempt: food and prescription drugs.

Local Sales Taxes (up to an additional %) 1.00

Inheritance Tax ....Yes
  Ranges from 0% to 15% depending on amount and the relationship of the recipient to the decedent.

Estate Tax.. No

PERSONAL INCOME TAXES

State Income Tax (%) ....0.36 - 8.98
  9 income brackets - Lowest $1,428; Highest $64,620. City and/or county income taxes not included.

Personal Exemption $ (single / joint) .... 40 / 80
  Amount is a tax credit.

Standard Deduction $ (single / joint)............1,810 / 4,460
Federal Income Tax Paid - Deduction Allowed ....Full

Social Security Income - Tax Exempt..........................Limits
Retired Military Pay - Tax Exempt ....Limits
State & Local Government Pensions - Tax Exempt .. Limits
Federal Civil Service Pensions - Tax Exempt .... Limits
Railroad Retirement - Tax Exempt ....Yes
Private Pension - Tax Exempt ....Limits

  Note: Limits include a maximum combined exemption of $24,000 (if 65 or older) from all retirement income sources including Social Security benefits.

VEHICLES

Registration Fees .... 1 Year
  Automobiles, trucks and multipurpose vehicles (SUV) registration fee is based on the weight, list price and age of vehicle. The minimum fee is $50.

  The formula is calculated as follows: 40 cents per hundred pounds of vehicle weight, plus....
  1% of list price on vehicles 1 to 7 years old
  3/4% of list price on vehicles 8 to 9 years old
  1/2% of list price on vehicles 10 to 11 years old
  Vehicles 12 model years old or more are a flat fee of $50.

  Travel trailer fees are 30 cents per square foot of floor space for vehicles under 7 model years old and 75% of total thereafter.

  Motor home fees are based on list price, age, and type. Class A, 1 to 5 years old, list price $80,000 and more, $400. Six years or older $300.

  Class A, 1 to 5 years old, list price $40,000 to $79,999, $200. Six years or older $150.

  Class A, 1 to 5 years old, list price $20,000 to $39,999, $140. Six years or older $105.

  Class A, 1 to 5 years old, list price less than $20,000, $120. Six years or older $85.

  Class B, 1 to 5 years old, $90. Six years or older $65.

  Class C, 1 to 5 years old, $110. Six years or older $80.00.

Annual Vehicle Tax ....Yes
  Fees are included in vehicle registration. No property tax on vehicles.

State Emissions Test Required .... No

Vehicle Safety Inspection Required .... No

Mandatory Minimum Liability Insurance 20/40/15

COST OF LIVING INDICATORS

Rank: 1 highest; 51 lowest

Cost of Living - average statewide (rank) 36
Per Capita Income (rank / $) .... 30 / 36,680
Median Household Income (rank / $) .... 30 / 49,007
Median House Value (rank / $).......................... 44 / 117,200
Median Property Tax on Homes (rank) 29
Fuel - avg per gal $, Mar 2010 (diesel / gas) ..... 2.81 / 2.65
Fuel Taxes - per gallon $ (diesel / gas)........... 0.479 / 0.404
Cigarette Tax - pack of 20 ($) 2.37
Tax Burden - average all taxes (rank) 32

STATE & LOCAL REVENUE SOURCES

Rank: 1 highest; 51 lowest
Rank and % of total revenue from:

Tax Revenue (see "Details" listed below) .... 32 / 39.51
Charges & Misc. Revenue.. 11 / 23.68
Federal Government .... 25 / 16.49
Utility Revenue.. 29 / 03.12
Insurance Trust Revenue.. 23 / 17.20

Tax Revenue Details (rank / %)

Property Tax.. 17 / 33.07
Sales & Gross Receipts .... 32 / 31.65
Individual Income Tax.. 21 / 25.07
Corporate Income Tax... 37 / 02.97
Motor Vehicle License.. 03 / 03.83
Other Taxes .... 43 / 03.41

POPULATION

Rank: 1 highest; 51 lowest

State Population (rank / count) .... 30 / 3,007,856
Population Per Square Mile (rank / count) .... 36 / 53

VOTING

Registration Requirements: In-person registration deadline is the day of election.

Address Requirements: Physical/street address required.

Register by Mail: Yes, registration deadline is 10 days before election.

Absentee Voting: Yes, no excuse is required.

Web Site: www.sos.state.ia.us/elections/

RESOURCES

Iowa State Government
Phone: 515-281-5011
Web Site: www.iowa.gov

Iowa Department of Revenue
Phone: 515-281-3114
Web Site: www.state.ia.us/tax

Iowa Motor Vehicle Division
Phone: 515-237-3110
Web Site: www.iowadot.gov/mvd and www.iowataxandtags.gov

Iowa Office of Tourism
Phone: 888-472-6035
Web Site: www.traveliowa.com

Kansas

WEATHER

	Topeka			Wichita		
	🌡	💧	❄	🌡	💧	❄
Jan	37/17	1	6.1	40/20	0.8	4.6
Feb	43/22	1.1	4.7	46/25	1	4.2
Mar	54/31	2.4	3.7	56/33	2.2	2.4
Apr	66/43	3.1	0.5	68/45	2.3	0.3
May	76/53	4.5	0	77/55	4	0
Jun	85/63	5.1	0	87/65	4.4	0
Jul	89/67	4.3	0	92/70	3.8	0
Aug	88/65	3.9	0	91/68	3	0
Sep	80/56	3.4	0	82/59	3.1	0
Oct	70/44	2.7	0	71/47	2.3	0
Nov	54/32	1.8	1.3	55/34	1.5	1.3
Dec	42/22	1.3	4.9	44/24	1	3.3

🌡	Average monthly high and low temperatures in degrees Fahrenheit.
💧	Average monthly precipitation totals in inches.
❄	Average monthly snowfall totals in inches.

STATE AND LOCAL TAXES

State Sales Tax (%) 5.30
   Exempt: prescription drugs. A sales tax refund on food is available to qualified residents.

Local Sales Taxes (up to an additional %) 3.00
Inheritance Tax .... No
Estate Tax.. No

PERSONAL INCOME TAXES

State Income Tax (%) .... 3.5 - 6.45
   3 income brackets - Lowest $15,000; Highest $30,000.

Personal Exemption $ (single / joint) ....2,250 / 4,500
Standard Deduction $ (single / joint)............3,000 / 6,000
   Additional $850 if age 65 or over.

Federal Income Tax Paid - Deduction Allowed .... None
Social Security Income - Tax Exempt........................... Limits
   Exempt if federal adjusted gross income is $75,000 or less.

Retired Military Pay - Tax Exempt ....Yes
State & Local Government Pensions - Tax Exempt .. Limits
   Full exemption for Kansas state pensions, none for out-of-state pensions.

Federal Civil Service Pensions - Tax Exempt ....Yes
Railroad Retirement - Tax Exempt ....Yes
Private Pension - Tax Exempt .... No

VEHICLES

Registration Fees .... 1 Year
   Basic fee for autos is $28 - $38, depending on weight of vehicle. Basic fee for trailers is $18 - $28, depending on weight.

Annual Vehicle Tax ....Yes
   Property tax due with vehicle registration. Rate varies by county.

State Emissions Test Required .... No
Vehicle Safety Inspection Required .... No
Mandatory Minimum Liability Insurance 25/50/10
   Personal Injury Protection, Uninsured and Underinsured Motorists coverage is also required.

COST OF LIVING INDICATORS

   Rank: 1 highest; 51 lowest

Cost of Living - average statewide (rank) 42
Per Capita Income (rank / $) .... 25 / 37,978
Median Household Income (rank / $) ....26 / 50,174
Median House Value (rank / $)........................42 / 120,200
Median Property Tax on Homes (rank) 27
Fuel - avg per gal $, Mar 2010 (diesel / gas).....2.78 / 2.61
Fuel Taxes - per gallon $ (diesel / gas)...........0.514 / 0.434
Cigarette Tax - pack of 20 ($) 1.80
Tax Burden - average all taxes (rank) 22

STATE & LOCAL REVENUE SOURCES

   Rank: 1 highest; 51 lowest
   Rank and % of total revenue from:

Tax Revenue (see "Details" listed below) ....05 / 47.99
Charges & Misc. Revenue..29 / 19.68
Federal Government ....38 / 14.17
Utility Revenue ....12 / 04.93
Insurance Trust Revenue..38 / 13.24

   Tax Revenue Details (rank / %)

Property Tax...21 / 30.46
Sales & Gross Receipts ....22 / 35.42
Individual Income Tax...23 / 24.19
Corporate Income Tax...21 / 04.65

Motor Vehicle License..26 / 01.58
Other Taxes ....39 / 03.70

POPULATION

Rank: 1 highest; 51 lowest

State Population (rank / count) .... 33 / 2,818,747
Population Per Square Mile (rank / count) .... 41 / 34

VOTING

Registration Requirements: In-person registration deadline is 15 days before election.

Address Requirements: Physical/street address required.

Register by Mail: Yes, registration deadline is 15 days before election.

Absentee Voting: Yes, no excuse is required.

Web Site: www.kssos.org/elections/elections.html

RESOURCES

Kansas State Government
Phone: 785-296-0111
Web Site: www.kansas.gov

Kansas Department of Revenue
Phone: 785-368-8222
Web Site: www.ksrevenue.org

Kansas Division of Motor Vehicles
Phone: 785-296-3621
Web Site: www.ksrevenue.org/vehicle.htm

Kansas Office of Tourism
Phone: 800-252-6727
Web Site: www.travelks.com

Kentucky

WEATHER

	Bowling Green			Louisville		
	🌡	💧	❄	🌡	💧	❄
Jan	47/28	5.2	3.3	41/25	3.4	5.1
Feb	49/29	4.1	2.8	46/28	3.4	4.5
Mar	60/37	5.1	1.7	56/36	4.5	3.2
Apr	71/46	4.3	0.2	68/46	4	0.1
May	80/55	4.2	0	77/55	4.5	0
Jun	88/63	4	0	85/64	3.6	0
Jul	91/67	4.2	0	88/68	4.2	0
Aug	90/66	3.6	0	87/66	3.3	0
Sep	85/59	3.1	0	80/59	3	0
Oct	73/47	2.7	0.1	69/47	2.6	0.1
Nov	59/36	3.8	0.5	56/37	3.7	1
Dec	48/29	4.3	2.1	45/29	3.5	2.2
🌡	Average monthly high and low temperatures in degrees Fahrenheit.					
💧	Average monthly precipitation totals in inches.					
❄	Average monthly snowfall totals in inches.					

STATE AND LOCAL TAXES

State Sales Tax (%) 6.00
Exempt: food and prescription drugs.

Local Sales Taxes (up to an additional %) .... None
Inheritance Tax ....Yes
Some beneficiaries are exempt from the tax.

Estate Tax...Yes
Limited.

PERSONAL INCOME TAXES

State Income Tax (%)...2 - 6
6 income brackets - Lowest $3,000; Highest $75,000. City and/or county income taxes not included.

Personal Exemption $ (single / joint) .... 20 / 40
Amount is a tax credit.

Standard Deduction $ (single / joint)............2,190 / 4,380
Can either itemize deductions or take the standard deduction.

Federal Income Tax Paid - Deduction Allowed .... None
Social Security Income - Tax Exempt .... Limits
Retired Military Pay - Tax Exempt .... Limits
State & Local Government Pensions - Tax Exempt .. Limits
Federal Civil Service Pensions - Tax Exempt .... Limits
Railroad Retirement - Tax Exempt .... Yes
Private Pension - Tax Exempt .... Limits

Note: Limits include a maximum combined exemption of $41,110 from all retirement income sources other than Railroad Retirement. Full exemption for benefits earned prior to 1/1/98.

VEHICLES

Registration Fees .... 1 Year
Basic fee, $15 plus. Other miscellaneous fees may apply, varies by county.

Note: A Motor Vehicle Usage Tax of 6% of the vehicles value is collected when registering a vehicle for the first time in Kentucky. A credit equal to the amount paid in another state will be applied to the amount owed in Kentucky.

Annual Vehicle Tax ....Yes
Property tax due with vehicle registration. Rate varies by county.

State Emissions Test Required .... No
Vehicle Safety Inspection Required .... No
Mandatory Minimum Liability Insurance 25/50/10
Personal Injury Protection is also required.

COST OF LIVING INDICATORS

Rank: 1 highest; 51 lowest

Cost of Living - average statewide (rank) 46
Per Capita Income (rank / $) .... 47 / 31,826
Median Household Income (rank / $) .... 48 / 41,489
Median House Value (rank / $)......................... 46 / 114,600
Median Property Tax on Homes (rank) 44
Fuel - avg per gal $, Mar 2010 (diesel / gas).....2.80 / 2.63
Fuel Taxes - per gallon $ (diesel / gas)...........0.439 / 0.409
Cigarette Tax - pack of 20 ($) 1.61
Tax Burden - average all taxes (rank) 26

STATE & LOCAL REVENUE SOURCES

Rank: 1 highest; 51 lowest
Rank and % of total revenue from:

Tax Revenue (see "Details" listed below) ....28 / 40.53
Charges & Misc. Revenue...31 / 19.31

Federal Government ....13 / 19.89
Utility Revenue...21 / 04.16
Insurance Trust Revenue...27 / 16.11

Tax Revenue Details (rank / %)

Property Tax..43 / 18.83
Sales & Gross Receipts ....20 / 37.09
Individual Income Tax..12 / 29.49
Corporate Income Tax..06 / 08.10
Motor Vehicle License...22 / 01.76
Other Taxes ....30 / 04.73

POPULATION

Rank: 1 highest; 51 lowest

State Population (rank / count) .... 26 / 4,314,113
Population Per Square Mile (rank / count) .... 22 / 107

VOTING

Registration Requirements: In-person registration deadline is 29 days before election.

Address Requirements: Physical/street address required.

Register by Mail: Yes, registration deadline is 29 days before election.

Absentee Voting: Yes, excuse required.

Web Site: www.elect.ky.gov/

RESOURCES

Kentucky State Government
Phone: 502-564-3130
Web Site: www.kentucky.gov

Kentucky Department of Revenue
Phone: 502-564-4581
Web Site: www.revenue.ky.gov

Kentucky Department of Vehicle Regulation
Phone: 502-564-7000
Web Site: www.transportation.ky.gov/dmc/home_vr.htm

Kentucky Office of Tourism
Phone: 800-225-8747
Web Site: www.kytourism.com

Louisiana

WEATHER

	New Orleans			Shreveport		
	🌡	💧	❄	🌡	💧	❄
Jan	62/43	5.1	N/A	56/36	4.1	0.8
Feb	65/46	5.5	N/A	61/39	4	0.5
Mar	71/52	5.3	N/A	69/46	3.7	0.2
Apr	78/58	4.8	N/A	77/54	4.6	0
May	85/66	4.9	N/A	83/62	5.1	0
Jun	89/71	5.6	N/A	90/70	4.1	0
Jul	91/73	6.6	N/A	93/73	3.6	0
Aug	90/73	5.9	N/A	93/72	2.5	0
Sep	87/70	5.4	N/A	88/66	3.1	0
Oct	80/60	2.8	N/A	79/55	3.7	0
Nov	71/50	4.5	N/A	67/45	4.1	0
Dec	65/45	5.3	N/A	59/38	4.2	0.2

🌡	Average monthly high and low temperatures in degrees Fahrenheit.
💧	Average monthly precipitation totals in inches.
❄	Average monthly snowfall totals in inches.

STATE AND LOCAL TAXES

State Sales Tax (%) 4.00
Exempt: food and prescription drugs.

Local Sales Taxes (up to an additional %) 6.75
Food is subject to local tax.

Inheritance Tax .... No
Estate Tax..Yes

PERSONAL INCOME TAXES

State Income Tax (%) ....2 - 6
3 income brackets - Lowest $12,500; Highest $50,000.

Personal Exemption $ (single / joint) ....4,500 / 9,000

Standard Deduction $ (single / joint)...........................None
Included in personal exemption.

Federal Income Tax Paid - Deduction Allowed ....Full

Social Security Income - Tax Exempt.................................Yes

Retired Military Pay - Tax Exempt ....Yes

State & Local Government Pensions - Tax Exempt .. Limits

Full exemption for Louisiana state pensions. For out-of-state pensions see Private Pension.

Federal Civil Service Pensions - Tax Exempt ....Yes

Railroad Retirement - Tax Exempt ....Yes

Private Pension - Tax Exempt ....Limits
Up to $6,000 exempt for taxpayers 65 or older.

VEHICLES

Registration Fees .... 2 Years
Autos, based on the value of the vehicle, $20 - $82.
Motor homes, $50.
Trucks, up to 6,000 lbs GVWR, $40. Fee is for 4 years.

New residents are subject to payment of a use tax of 4% based on the value of the vehicle. A maximum of 4% credit may be allowed for a similar tax paid in another state.

Annual Vehicle Tax .... No
No property tax on vehicles.

State Emissions Test Required ....Yes
Annual in the five-parish Baton Rouge area consisting of Ascension, East Baton Rouge, Iberville, Livingston, and West Baton Rouge parishes. Diesel powered and all other vehicles over 10,000 lbs GVWR are exempt. Web Site: www.deq.state.la.us/portal/tabid/110/Default.aspx.

Vehicle Safety Inspection Required ....Yes
Every two years.

Mandatory Minimum Liability Insurance 15/30/25

COST OF LIVING INDICATORS

Rank: 1 highest; 51 lowest

Cost of Living - average statewide (rank) 30
Per Capita Income (rank / $) ....31 / 36,271
Median Household Income (rank / $) ....44 / 43,635
Median House Value (rank / $).....................38 / 123,900
Median Property Tax on Homes (rank) 51
Fuel - avg per gal $, Mar 2010 (diesel / gas) .....2.77 / 2.62
Fuel Taxes - per gallon $ (diesel / gas)...........0.444 / 0.384
Cigarette Tax - pack of 20 ($) 1.37
Tax Burden - average all taxes (rank) 43

STATE & LOCAL REVENUE SOURCES

Rank: 1 highest; 51 lowest
Rank and % of total revenue from:

Tax Revenue (see "Details" listed below) ....41 / 37.58

Charges & Misc. Revenue..35 / 18.21

Federal Government ....02 / 28.41

Utility Revenue...31 / 02.60

Insurance Trust Revenue..........................39 / 13.21

Tax Revenue Details (rank / %)

Property Tax..49 / 14.84

Sales & Gross Receipts ....06 / 53.09

Individual Income Tax...............................36 / 18.27

Corporate Income Tax...............................24 / 04.28

Motor Vehicle License ....43 / 00.64

Other Taxes ....17 / 08.88

POPULATION

Rank: 1 highest; 51 lowest

State Population (rank / count) ....25 / 4,492,076

Population Per Square Mile (rank / count) ....27 / 87

VOTING

Registration Requirements: In-person registration deadline is 30 days before election.

Address Requirements: Physical/street address required.

Register by Mail: Yes, registration deadline is 30 days before election.

Absentee Voting: Yes, excuse required.

Web Site: www.sos.louisiana.gov/tabid/68/Default.aspx

RESOURCES

Louisiana State Government
Phone: 800-354-9548
Web Site: www.louisiana.gov

Louisiana Department of Revenue
Phone: 225-219-2448
Web Site: www.rev.state.la.us

Louisiana Office of Motor Vehicles
Phone: 877-368-5463
Web Site: http://omv.dps.state.la.us

Louisiana Office of Tourism
Phone: 800-994-8626
Web Site: www.louisianatravel.com

Maine

WEATHER

	Bangor			Portland		
	🌡	💧	❄	🌡	💧	❄
Jan	28/10	3.9	23	31/12	3.7	19
Feb	31/12	3.8	26	33/14	3.3	17.4
Mar	39/22	3.9	18.4	41/24	4	13
Apr	52/34	3.4	4.3	53/34	3.9	3.1
May	64/43	3.2	0.3	63/43	3.6	0.2
Jun	73/52	2.9	0	73/52	3.1	0
Jul	78/58	3.8	0	79/58	2.9	0
Aug	77/56	2.7	0	78/56	2.9	0
Sep	69/49	3.7	0	69/48	3.2	0
Oct	57/39	3.9	0.9	59/38	3.6	0.2
Nov	45/30	4.7	7	47/30	5	3
Dec	32/16	4.1	17.4	36/18	4.3	14.6

🌡	Average monthly high and low temperatures in degrees Fahrenheit.
💧	Average monthly precipitation totals in inches.
❄	Average monthly snowfall totals in inches.

STATE AND LOCAL TAXES

State Sales Tax (%)...5.00
Exempt: food and prescription drugs.

Local Sales Taxes (up to an additional %) ....None

Inheritance Tax .... No

Estate Tax...Yes
On estates valued at $1 million or more.

PERSONAL INCOME TAXES

State Income Tax (%) ....2 - 6.85
2 income brackets - Lowest $5,050; Highest $250,000.

Personal Exemption $ (single / joint) ....2,850 / 5,700

Standard Deduction $ (single / joint)............5,700 / 9,550

Federal Income Tax Paid - Deduction Allowed.......... None

Social Security Income - Tax Exempt................................Yes

Retired Military Pay - Tax Exempt .... Limits

State & Local Government Pensions - Tax Exempt .. Limits

Federal Civil Service Pensions - Tax Exempt .... Limits

Railroad Retirement - Tax Exempt ....Yes

Private Pension - Tax Exempt ....Limits

> Note: Limits include a maximum combined exemption of $6,000 from all retirement income sources including Social Security and Railroad Retirement.

VEHICLES

Registration Fees .... 1 Year
Passenger vehicle, $35.
Truck camper, $12.
Motor homes, based on weight:
0 - 16,000 lbs, $21 - $50.
16,001 - 26,000 lbs, $72 - $119.
26,001 - 28,000 lbs, $137 - $166.
28,001 - 38,000 lbs, $166 - $265.
38,001 - 60,000 lbs, $276 - $394.

Annual Vehicle Tax ....Yes
An annual excise tax is paid to the town like a property tax and is based on the age and vehicle MSRP. To estimate your cost, multiply the MSRP by the mill rate shown below:
Year 1 - .0240 mill rate
Year 2 - .0175 mill rate
Year 3 - .0135 mill rate
Year 4 - .0100 mill rate
Year 5 - .0065 mill rate
Year 6 - .0040 mill rate

State Emissions Test Required ....Yes
In Cumberland County only. Diesel powered vehicles under 18,000 lbs are exempt. Web Site: www.maine.gov/dep/air/mobile/enhancedautoinsp.htm

Vehicle Safety Inspection Required ....Yes
Annual.

Mandatory Minimum Liability Insurance 50/100/25
Uninsured and Underinsured Motorists coverage required. There is also a mandatory $1,000 medical payments coverage.

COST OF LIVING INDICATORS

> Rank: 1 highest; 51 lowest

Cost of Living - average statewide (rank) 13
Per Capita Income (rank / $) .... 34 / 35,381
Median Household Income (rank / $) .... 38 / 46,419
Median House Value (rank / $).........................24 / 175,200
Median Property Tax on Homes (rank) 21
Fuel - avg per gal $, Mar 2010 (diesel / gas) .....3.05 / 2.74
Fuel Taxes - per gallon $ (diesel / gas)...........0.566 / 0.494
Cigarette Tax - pack of 20 ($) 3.01
Tax Burden - average all taxes (rank) 16

STATE & LOCAL REVENUE SOURCES

> Rank: 1 highest; 51 lowest
> Rank and % of total revenue from:

Tax Revenue (see "Details" listed below) ....13 / 45.51
Charges & Misc. Revenue..44 / 16.95
Federal Government ....10 / 20.40
Utility Revenue ....47 / 00.92
Insurance Trust Revenue..25 / 16.22

> *Tax Revenue Details (rank / %)*

Property Tax...11 / 36.58
Sales & Gross Receipts ....35 / 30.07
Individual Income Tax...24 / 24.13
Corporate Income Tax...33 / 03.27
Motor Vehicle License ....27 / 01.57
Other Taxes ....35 / 04.38

POPULATION

> Rank: 1 highest; 51 lowest

State Population (rank / count) .... 41 / 1,318,301
Population Per Square Mile (rank / count) .... 40 / 37

VOTING

Registration Requirements: In-person registration deadline is the day of election.

Address Requirements: Physical/street address required.

Register by Mail: Yes, registration deadline is the 21st day before election.

Absentee Voting: Yes, no excuse is required.

Web Site: www.maine.gov/sos/cec/elec/

RESOURCES

Maine State Government
Phone: 207-624-9494
Web Site: www.maine.gov

Maine Revenue Services
Phone: 207-626-8475
Web Site: www.maine.gov/revenue

Maine Bureau of Motor Vehicles
Phone: 207-624-9000
Web Site: www.state.me.us/sos/bmv

Maine Office of Tourism
Phone: 888-624-6345
Web Site: www.visitmaine.com

Maryland

WEATHER

	Baltimore			Cumberland		
	🌡	💧	❄	🌡	💧	❄
Jan	41/24	3	5.9	41/25	2.7	4.5
Feb	44/26	3	6.5	45/26	2.5	4.2
Mar	53/34	3.8	3.8	51/30	3.6	7.3
Apr	65/43	3.1	0.1	66/42	3.5	0.7
May	74/53	3.6	0	75/50	4.1	0
Jun	83/62	3.5	0	82/58	4.5	0
Jul	88/67	3.8	0	87/62	3.5	0
Aug	85/66	4	0	85/61	3.7	0
Sep	79/58	3.5	0	78/54	2.7	0
Oct	68/46	3	0	68/44	2.7	0
Nov	56/37	3.2	1	53/34	2.6	1.5
Dec	45/28	3.3	3.5	42/25	2.4	4.4

🌡	Average monthly high and low temperatures in degrees Fahrenheit.
💧	Average monthly precipitation totals in inches.
❄	Average monthly snowfall totals in inches.

STATE AND LOCAL TAXES

State Sales Tax (%)..6.00
  Exempt: food and prescription drugs.

Local Sales Taxes (up to an additional %) .... None

Inheritance Tax ....Yes
  Some beneficiaries are exempt from the tax.

Estate Tax..Yes
  On estates valued at $1 million or more. Limited to federal estate tax collection.

PERSONAL INCOME TAXES

State Income Tax (%)......................................2 - 6.25
  8 income brackets - Lowest $1,000; Highest $1,000,000. City and/or county income taxes not included.

Personal Exemption $ (single / joint) ....3,200 / 6,400
  The exemption amount declines in 5 income brackets starting at $100,000 for single and $150,000 for joint

returns. *The first income bracket takes the exemption to $2,400 and down to $600 in the fifth bracket with income in excess of $200,000 or $250,000 for joint returns.*

Standard Deduction $ (single / joint)............1,500 / 3,000
  Or 15% of Maryland adjusted gross income to maximum of $3,000 for single returns and maximum of $3,000 to $4,000 for joint returns.

Federal Income Tax Paid - Deduction Allowed .... None

Social Security Income - Tax Exempt ....Yes

Retired Military Pay - Tax Exempt .... Limits

State & Local Government Pensions - Tax Exempt .. Limits

Federal Civil Service Pensions - Tax Exempt .... Limits

Railroad Retirement - Tax Exempt ....Yes

Private Pension - Tax Exempt .... Limits

  Note: If you are 65 or older you may qualify for a pension exclusion (maximum $23,600) under certain conditions. Out-of-state government pensions do not qualify for the exemption.

VEHICLES

Registration Fees .... 2 Years
  Passenger and multi purpose vehicles including RVs up to 3,700 lbs, $128.

  Passenger and multi purpose vehicles including RVs over 3,700 lbs, $180.

  Trucks, 3/4 ton or 7,000 lbs or less, $154.50.
  Trucks, 10,000 lbs GVW (1/2 or 3/4 ton), $207.

  Trailers 3,000 lbs or less, $51.
  Trailers 3,001 - 5,000 lbs, $102.
  Trailers 5,001 - 10,000 lbs, $160.
  Trailers 10,001 - 20,000 lbs, 248.

  Note: You must register your vehicle within 60 days of moving to Maryland. If you do not, you will not be eligible for a tax credit for any titling tax paid in another state. Vehicles titled in a state with a tax rate equal to or higher than Maryland's 6% rate will cost $100. If the other state imposes no tax, the tax will be assessed at 6% of the vehicles value. If the other state has a lower tax rate you will be taxed for the difference. Minimum tax is $100.

Annual Vehicle Tax .... No
  No property tax on vehicles.

State Emissions Test Required ....Yes
  Every 2 years. Tests vary with year and weight of vehicle.

The "Diesel Vehicle Emissions Program" requires testing for vehicles over 10,000 lbs. Web Site: www.mva.maryland.gov/MVAProg/VEIP/default.htm

Vehicle Safety Inspection Required ....Yes
Annual. Required before a vehicle can be registered.

Mandatory Minimum Liability Insurance 20/40/15
Personal Injury Protection, Uninsured and Underinsured Motorists coverage is also required.

COST OF LIVING INDICATORS

Rank: 1 highest; 51 lowest

Cost of Living - average statewide (rank) 06
Per Capita Income (rank / $) ....06 / 48,091
Median Household Income (rank / $) ....01 / 70,482
Median House Value (rank / $) ....06 / 340,900
Median Property Tax on Homes (rank) 11
Fuel - avg per gal $, Mar 2010 (diesel / gas) .....2.91 / 2.68
Fuel Taxes - per gallon $ (diesel / gas) ....0.487 / 0.419
Cigarette Tax - pack of 20 ($) 3.01
Tax Burden - average all taxes (rank) 04

STATE & LOCAL REVENUE SOURCES

Rank: 1 highest; 51 lowest
Rank and % of total revenue from:

Tax Revenue (see "Details" listed below) ....03 / 50.17
Charges & Misc. Revenue...46 / 16.38
Federal Government ....34 / 14.99
Utility Revenue ....45 / 01.29
Insurance Trust Revenue...24 / 17.18

Tax Revenue Details (rank / %)

Property Tax...36 / 24.19
Sales & Gross Receipts ....45 / 23.40
Individual Income Tax..02 / 39.70
Corporate Income Tax...38 / 02.89
Motor Vehicle License...23 / 01.70
Other Taxes ....19 / 08.12

POPULATION

Rank: 1 highest; 51 lowest

State Population (rank / count) ....19 / 5,699,478
Population Per Square Mile (rank / count) ....06 / 459

VOTING

Registration Requirements: In-person registration deadline is 21 days before election.

Address Requirements: Physical/street address required.

Register by Mail: Yes, registration deadline is 21 days before election.

Absentee Voting: Yes, excuse required.

Web Site: www.elections.state.md.us/

RESOURCES

Maryland State Government
Phone: 877-634-6361
Web Site: www.maryland.gov

Comptroller of Maryland
Phone: 800-638-2937
Web Site: www.marylandtaxes.com

Maryland Motor Vehicle Administration
Phone: 800-950-1682
Web Site: www.mva.state.md.us

Maryland Office of Tourism
Phone: 866-639-3526
Web Site: www.mdisfun.org

Massachusetts

WEATHER

	Boston			Springfield		
	🌡	💧	❄	🌡	💧	❄
Jan	36/22	3.8	12	33/16	3.2	13.6
Feb	38/23	3.5	11.3	35/18	3	11.8
Mar	45/31	4	7.9	45/28	3.4	8.7
Apr	56/40	3.7	0.9	58/37	3.7	1.6
May	67/50	3.4	0	70/47	3.8	0.1
Jun	77/59	3	0	78/56	3.7	0
Jul	82/65	2.8	0	83/61	3.8	0
Aug	80/64	3.6	0	81/59	3.6	0
Sep	73/57	3.3	0	73/51	3.4	0
Oct	63/47	3.3	0	63/40	3.1	0.1
Nov	52/38	4.4	1.3	50/32	3.9	2.5
Dec	41/27	4.2	7.5	37/21	3.5	11

🌡	Average monthly high and low temperatures in degrees Fahrenheit.
💧	Average monthly precipitation totals in inches.
❄	Average monthly snowfall totals in inches.

STATE AND LOCAL TAXES

State Sales Tax (%) 6.25
Exempt: food and prescription drugs.

Local Sales Taxes (up to an additional %) .... None
Inheritance Tax .... No
Estate Tax...Yes
On estates valued at $1 million or more.

PERSONAL INCOME TAXES

State Income Tax (%) 5.3
Flat rate, no income brackets. A 12% tax rate applies to short-term capital gains. Taxpayers have the choice of paying an optional higher rate of 5.85%.

Personal Exemption $ (single / joint) ....4,400 / 8,800
Standard Deduction $ (single / joint)........................... None
Federal Income Tax Paid - Deduction Allowed .... None
Social Security Income - Tax Exempt...............................Yes
Retired Military Pay - Tax Exempt ....Yes

State & Local Government Pensions - Tax Exempt .. Limits
Full exemption for Massachusetts state pensions and some out-of-state pensions.

Federal Civil Service Pensions - Tax Exempt ....Yes
Railroad Retirement - Tax Exempt ....Yes
Private Pension - Tax Exempt .... No

VEHICLES

Registration Fees ....1 & 2 Years
Passenger vehicles, $50. For two years.
Motor homes, $50. For one year.

Annual Vehicle Tax ....Yes
An annual Motor Vehicle Excise Tax is levied by the city or town. The rate is $25 per $1,000 of valuation. Age and list price (in year of manufacture) is used to figure the valuation. For detailed information see: www.sec.state. ma.us/cis/cisexc/excidx.htm.
50% - In the year preceding the model year (brand new car released before model year).
90% - In the model year.
60% - In the second year.
40% - In the third year.
25% - In the fourth year.
10% - In the fifth and succeeding years.

State Emissions Test Required ....Yes
Annual. Vehicle safety inspection and emissions test are done at the same time. Web Site: http://massvehiclecheck. state.ma.us/index.html

Vehicle Safety Inspection Required ....Yes
Annual.

Mandatory Minimum Liability Insurance 20/40/5
Personal Injury Protection and Uninsured Motorist coverage is also required.

COST OF LIVING INDICATORS

Rank: 1 highest; 51 lowest

Cost of Living - average statewide (rank) 11
Per Capita Income (rank / $) ....04 / 50,735
Median Household Income (rank / $) ....06 / 65,304
Median House Value (rank / $)........................05 / 363,900
Median Property Tax on Homes (rank) 06
Fuel - avg per gal $, Mar 2010 (diesel / gas).....2.95 / 2.69
Fuel Taxes - per gallon $ (diesel / gas)...........0.479 / 0.419
Cigarette Tax - pack of 20 ($) 3.52
Tax Burden - average all taxes (rank) 24

STATE & LOCAL REVENUE SOURCES

Rank: 1 highest; 51 lowest
Rank and % of total revenue from:

Tax Revenue (see "Details" listed below) ....11 / 45.70
Charges & Misc. Revenue..................................42 / 17.26
Federal Government ....33 / 15.16
Utility Revenue..20 / 04.23
Insurance Trust Revenue...................................22 / 17.76

Tax Revenue Details (rank / %)

Property Tax..13 / 34.38
Sales & Gross Receipts ....46 / 19.21
Individual Income Tax.......................................03 / 35.49
Corporate Income Tax.......................................08 / 06.56
Motor Vehicle License.......................................40 / 00.94
Other Taxes ....42 / 03.42

POPULATION

Rank: 1 highest; 51 lowest

State Population (rank / count) ....15 / 6,593,587
Population Per Square Mile (rank / count) ....05 / 625

VOTING

Registration Requirements: In-person registration deadline is 20 days before election.

Address Requirements: Physical/street address required.

Register by Mail: Yes, registration deadline is 20 days before election.

Absentee Voting: Yes, excuse required.

Web Site: www.sec.state.ma.us/ele/eleidx.htm

RESOURCES

Massachusetts State Government
Phone: 866-888-2808
Web Site: www.mass.gov

Massachusetts Department of Revenue
Phone: 617-887-6367
Web Site: www.dor.state.ma.us

Massachusetts Registry of Motor Vehicles
Phone: 617-351-4500
Web Site: www.massdot.state.ma.us/rmv

Massachusetts Office of Tourism
Phone: 800-227-6277
Web Site: www.massvacation.com

Michigan

WEATHER

	Detroit			Sault Ste. Marie		
	🌡	💧	❄	🌡	💧	❄
Jan	31/16	1.9	10.2	22/5	2.3	28.7
Feb	33/18	1.7	9.1	24/6	1.6	18.7
Mar	44/27	2.4	7	33/15	2.1	14.8
Apr	58/37	3	1.7	47/29	2.5	5.6
May	70/48	2.9	0	62/38	2.6	0.5
Jun	79/57	3.6	0	70/46	3.2	0
Jul	83/62	3.1	0	76/52	2.9	0
Aug	81/60	3.4	0	74/52	3.3	0
Sep	74/53	2.8	0	64/45	3.8	0.1
Oct	62/41	2.2	0.2	54/37	3.1	2.5
Nov	48/32	2.7	3	39/26	3.4	15.3
Dec	35/22	2.5	10.2	27/13	2.7	29.9
🌡	Average monthly high and low temperatures in degrees Fahrenheit.					
💧	Average monthly precipitation totals in inches.					
❄	Average monthly snowfall totals in inches.					

STATE AND LOCAL TAXES

State Sales Tax (%) 6.00
  Exempt: food and prescription drugs.

Local Sales Taxes (up to an additional %) .... None
Inheritance Tax .... No
Estate Tax..Yes
  Limited to federal estate tax collection.

PERSONAL INCOME TAXES

State Income Tax (%) 4.35
  Flat rate, no income brackets. City and/or county income taxes not included.

Personal Exemption $ (single / joint) ....3,500 / 7,000
  Additional $2,200 if age 65 or over.

Standard Deduction $ (single / joint)............................None
Federal Income Tax Paid - Deduction Allowed ....None
Social Security Income - Tax Exempt.................................Yes

Retired Military Pay - Tax Exempt ....Yes

State & Local Government Pensions - Tax Exempt ..Limits
Full exemption for Michigan state pensions and some out-of-state pensions.

Federal Civil Service Pensions - Tax Exempt ....Yes

Railroad Retirement - Tax Exempt ....Yes

Private Pension - Tax Exempt .... Limits
Exempt up to $42,240, some restrictions.

VEHICLES

Registration Fees .... 1 Year
Fees for 1984 or newer passenger vehicles and light trucks are calculated using a percentage of the manufacturer's suggested retail price at the time the vehicle is first titled. This amount is known as the base price. It is then reduced by a percentage of that registration fee for the following three years.

If the vehicle is older than 1984, the fee is based on the weight of the vehicle.

You can call the Record Information Unit at 1-888-767-6424 for an estimate on total fees.

Annual Vehicle Tax ....Yes
Fees are included in vehicle registration. No property tax on vehicles.

State Emissions Test Required .... No

Vehicle Safety Inspection Required .... No

Mandatory Minimum Liability Insurance 20/40/10
Personal Injury Protection is also required.

COST OF LIVING INDICATORS

Rank: 1 highest; 51 lowest

Cost of Living - average statewide (rank) 28

Per Capita Income (rank / $) .... 35 / 35,299

Median Household Income (rank / $) .... 31 / 48,606

Median House Value (rank / $).........................32 / 152,600

Median Property Tax on Homes (rank) 17

Fuel - avg per gal $, Mar 2010 (diesel / gas).....2.85 / 2.64

Fuel Taxes - per gallon $ (diesel / gas)...........0.403 / 0.383
Plus state sales tax.

Cigarette Tax - pack of 20 ($) 3.01

Tax Burden - average all taxes (rank) 28

STATE & LOCAL REVENUE SOURCES

Rank: 1 highest; 51 lowest
Rank and % of total revenue from:

Tax Revenue (see "Details" listed below) ....29 / 40.05

Charges & Misc. Revenue...10 / 24.08

Federal Government ....31 / 15.54

Utility Revenue...34 / 02.38

Insurance Trust Revenue..20 / 17.96

Tax Revenue Details (rank / %)

Property Tax...06 / 39.19

Sales & Gross Receipts ....30 / 32.03

Individual Income Tax...35 / 18.63

Corporate Income Tax...18 / 04.82

Motor Vehicle License...13 / 02.45

Other Taxes ....48 / 02.88

POPULATION

Rank: 1 highest; 51 lowest

State Population (rank / count) ....08 / 9,969,727

Population Per Square Mile (rank / count) ....23 / 103

VOTING

Registration Requirements: In-person registration deadline is 30 days before election.

Address Requirements: Physical/street address required.

Register by Mail: Yes, registration deadline is 30 days before election.

Absentee Voting: Yes, excuse required.

Web Site: https://webapps.sos.state.mi.us/mivote/

RESOURCES

Michigan State Government
Phone: 517-373-1837
Web Site: www.michigan.gov

Michigan Department of Treasury
Phone: 517-373-3200
Web Site: www.michigan.gov/treasury

Michigan Department of State (Vehicle Registration)
Phone: 888-767-6424
Web Site: www.michigan.gov/sos

Michigan Office of Tourism
Phone: 888-784-7328
Web Site: www.michigan.org

Minnesota

WEATHER

	Duluth			Minneapolis		
	🌡	💧	❄	🌡	💧	❄
Jan	16/-1	1.2	16.8	21/4	0.8	9.8
Feb	22/3	0.8	11.2	27/9	0.8	8.4
Mar	32/15	1.8	13.3	39/22	1.8	10.7
Apr	48/29	2.4	6.5	56/36	2.2	2.8
May	62/40	3.2	0.8	69/48	3.1	0.1
Jun	71/48	4.1	0	78/58	4.1	0
Jul	76/54	4	0	83/63	3.7	0
Aug	74/53	3.9	0	81/61	3.6	0
Sep	64/45	3.6	0.1	71/50	2.7	0
Oct	53/35	2.4	1.4	59/40	1.9	0.5
Nov	35/21	1.9	12.5	40/25	1.5	7.9
Dec	22/6	1.3	15.4	26/11	1	9.3

🌡	Average monthly high and low temperatures in degrees Fahrenheit.
💧	Average monthly precipitation totals in inches.
❄	Average monthly snowfall totals in inches.

STATE AND LOCAL TAXES

State Sales Tax (%) 6.875
Exempt: food and prescription drugs.

Local Sales Taxes (up to an additional %) 2.50
Inheritance Tax .... No
Estate Tax .... Yes
Limited to federal estate tax collection.

PERSONAL INCOME TAXES

State Income Tax (%) .... 5.35 - 7.85
3 income brackets - Lowest $22,730; Highest $74,650.

Personal Exemption $ (single / joint) .... 3,500 / 7,000
Standard Deduction $ (single / joint) .... 5,450 / 10,900
Federal Income Tax Paid - Deduction Allowed .... None
Social Security Income - Tax Exempt .... Limits
Taxed same as on your federal return. No tax if Social Security is your only income.

Retired Military Pay - Tax Exempt .... No
State & Local Government Pensions - Tax Exempt .... No
Federal Civil Service Pensions - Tax Exempt .... No
Railroad Retirement - Tax Exempt .... Yes
Private Pension - Tax Exempt .... No

VEHICLES

Registration Fees .... 1 Year
Basic fee, $22 plus. Varies with type of vehicle and miscellaneous additional charges.

Annual Vehicle Tax .... Yes
An annual "Registration Tax" is determined by the age and value of the vehicle. Minimum tax for vehicles 10 years old or older is $35. Contact Driver and Vehicle Services for assistance in determining the total tax amount.

State Emissions Test Required .... No
Vehicle Safety Inspection Required .... No
Mandatory Minimum Liability Insurance 30/60/10
Personal Injury Protection, Uninsured Motorist, and Underinsured Motorists coverage is also required.

COST OF LIVING INDICATORS

Rank: 1 highest; 51 lowest

Cost of Living - average statewide (rank) 20
Per Capita Income (rank / $) .... 11 / 42,772
Median Household Income (rank / $) .... 13 / 57,318
Median House Value (rank / $) .... 21 / 212,100
Median Property Tax on Homes (rank) 20
Fuel - avg per gal $, Mar 2010 (diesel / gas) ..... 2.90 / 2.69
Fuel Taxes - per gallon $ (diesel / gas) .... 0.516 / 0.456
Cigarette Tax - pack of 20 ($) 2.57
Tax Burden - average all taxes (rank) 13

STATE & LOCAL REVENUE SOURCES

Rank: 1 highest; 51 lowest
Rank and % of total revenue from:

Tax Revenue (see "Details" listed below) .... 17 / 43.54
Charges & Misc. Revenue .... 27 / 19.72
Federal Government .... 41 / 13.49
Utility Revenue .... 28 / 03.21
Insurance Trust Revenue .... 12 / 20.03

Tax Revenue Details (rank / %)

Property Tax .... 34 / 25.86
Sales & Gross Receipts .... 31 / 31.81
Individual Income Tax .... 08 / 30.56

Corporate Income Tax..16 / 05.00
Motor Vehicle License...15 / 02.18
Other Taxes ....33 / 04.59

POPULATION

Rank: 1 highest; 51 lowest

State Population (rank / count) ....21 / 5,266,214
Population Per Square Mile (rank / count) ....32 / 61

VOTING

Registration Requirements: In-person registration deadline is the day of election.

Address Requirements: Physical/street address required.

Register by Mail: Yes, registration deadline is 20 days before election.

Absentee Voting: Yes, excuse required.

Web Site: www.sos.state.mn.us/home/index.asp

RESOURCES

Minnesota State Government
Phone: 651-296-1424
Web Site: www.state.mn.us

Minnesota Department of Revenue
Phone: 651-296-3781
Web Site: www.taxes.state.mn.us

Minnesota Driver and Vehicle Services
Phone: 651-297-2126
Web Site: www.dps.state.mn.us/dvs

Minnesota Office of Tourism
Phone: 800-657-3700
Web Site: www.exploreminnesota.com

Mississippi

WEATHER

	Jackson			Tupelo		
	🌡	💧	❄	🌡	💧	❄
Jan	56/34	5.1	0.5	50/32	3.4	1.4
Feb	60/37	4.6	0.2	56/36	5.7	0.8
Mar	69/45	5.7	0.2	65/43	4.8	0.3
Apr	77/52	5.9	0	74/50	4.1	0
May	83/61	5.2	0	81/60	5.6	0
Jun	90/68	3.3	0	88/67	4.7	0
Jul	92/71	4.6	0	91/71	2.8	0
Aug	92/70	3.9	0	91/70	3	0
Sep	87/65	3.5	0	85/63	3	0
Oct	78/52	3.4	0	74/51	3.7	0
Nov	68/43	4.7	0	63/42	5	0
Dec	59/37	5.6	0	53/35	6.2	0.4

🌡	Average monthly high and low temperatures in degrees Fahrenheit.
💧	Average monthly precipitation totals in inches.
❄	Average monthly snowfall totals in inches.

STATE AND LOCAL TAXES

State Sales Tax (%)..7.00
Exempt: prescription drugs.

Local Sales Taxes (up to an additional %) 4.50
Inheritance Tax ....No
Estate Tax..Yes
On estates valued at $1 million or more.

PERSONAL INCOME TAXES

State Income Tax (%)...3 - 5
3 income brackets - Lowest $5,000; Highest $10,000.

Personal Exemption $ (single / joint) ....6,000 / 12,000
Additional $1,500 if age 65 or over.

Standard Deduction $ (single / joint)............2,300 / 4,600
Federal Income Tax Paid - Deduction Allowed..........None
Social Security Income - Tax Exempt...................................Yes
Retired Military Pay - Tax Exempt ....Yes

State & Local Government Pensions - Tax Exempt ....Yes
Federal Civil Service Pensions - Tax Exempt ....Yes
Railroad Retirement - Tax Exempt ....Yes
Private Pension - Tax Exempt ....Limits
   Exempt for qualified plans.

VEHICLES

Registration Fees .... 1 Year
   Basic fee, $12.75. A Privilege Tax is due in addition to the basic fee: Passenger vehicles $15.00, trailers $10.00, pickup trucks $7.20.

Annual Vehicle Tax ....Yes
   Motor Vehicle Ad Valorem Tax. Vehicles with a GVWR of 10,000 lbs or less must pay this tax at the time of registration. The tax is based on the assessed value of the vehicle multiplied by the millage rate set by local county government.

   Assessed value has been established as 30% of MSRP plus a reduction of a certain percentage for depreciation over 10 years. There is a minimum assessed value of $100. Contact the local county tax collector for their millage rate and depreciation factor.

State Emissions Test Required .... No
Vehicle Safety Inspection Required ....Yes
   Annual.
Mandatory Minimum Liability Insurance 25/50/25

COST OF LIVING INDICATORS
   Rank: 1 highest; 51 lowest

Cost of Living - average statewide (rank) 38
Per Capita Income (rank / $) ....51 / 29,569
Median Household Income (rank / $) ....50 / 37,818
Median House Value (rank / $)............................50 / 94,000
Median Property Tax on Homes (rank) 48
Fuel - avg per gal $, Mar 2010 (diesel / gas) .....2.76 / 2.61
Fuel Taxes - per gallon $ (diesel / gas)............0.428 / 0.368
   Local fees may add up to 3 cents.
Cigarette Tax - pack of 20 ($) 1.69
Tax Burden - average all taxes (rank) 37

STATE & LOCAL REVENUE SOURCES
   Rank: 1 highest; 51 lowest
   Rank and % of total revenue from:

Tax Revenue (see "Details" listed below) ....51 / 29.50
Charges & Misc. Revenue...34 / 18.60
Federal Government ....01 / 33.06

Utility Revenue ....30 / 02.73
Insurance Trust Revenue...28 / 16.10

   Tax Revenue Details (rank / %)

Property Tax...35 / 25.27
Sales & Gross Receipts ....10 / 47.90
Individual Income Tax..39 / 16.05
Corporate Income Tax...25 / 04.23
Motor Vehicle License...30 / 01.43
Other Taxes ....28 / 05.12

POPULATION
   Rank: 1 highest; 51 lowest

State Population (rank / count) ....31 / 2,951,996
Population Per Square Mile (rank / count) .... 33 / 61

VOTING

Registration Requirements: In-person registration deadline is 30 days before election.

Address Requirements: Physical/street address required.

Register by Mail: Yes, registration deadline is 30 days before election.

Absentee Voting: Yes, excuse required.

Web Site: www.sos.state.ms.us/elections/elections.asp

RESOURCES

Mississippi State Government
Phone: 601-359-1000
Web Site: www.ms.gov

Mississippi State Tax Commission (Taxes & Vehicle Registration)
Phone: 601-923-7000
Web Site: www.mstc.state.ms.us

Mississippi Department of Public Safety (Drivers License)
Phone: 601-987-1212
Web Site: www.dps.state.ms.us

Mississippi Office of Tourism
Phone: 866-733-6477
Web Site: www.visitmississippi.org

Missouri

WEATHER

	Kansas City			Saint Louis		
	🌡	💧	❄	🌡	💧	❄
Jan	39/21	1.3	5.8	39/21	2	5.3
Feb	43/25	1.3	4.5	44/25	2.1	4.7
Mar	54/34	2.5	3.6	54/34	3.3	4.2
Apr	66/46	3.3	0.8	67/46	3.6	0.4
May	75/56	4.5	0	76/55	3.9	0
Jun	84/66	4.8	0	85/65	3.8	0
Jul	90/71	3.7	0	89/69	3.8	0
Aug	88/69	3.9	0	87/67	3	0
Sep	80/61	4.3	0	80/59	3	0
Oct	69/49	3	0	69/48	2.8	0
Nov	54/36	1.9	1.1	54/36	3.1	1.4
Dec	42/26	1.5	4.4	43/26	2.6	3.8
🌡	Average monthly high and low temperatures in degrees Fahrenheit.					
💧	Average monthly precipitation totals in inches.					
❄	Average monthly snowfall totals in inches.					

STATE AND LOCAL TAXES

State Sales Tax (%) 4.225
Prescription drugs exempt. Food is taxed at 1.225%.

Local Sales Taxes (up to an additional %) 5.375
Inheritance Tax .... No
Estate Tax .... No

PERSONAL INCOME TAXES

State Income Tax (%) .... 1.5 - 6
10 income brackets - Lowest $1,000; Highest $9,000. City and/or county income taxes not included.

Personal Exemption $ (single / joint) ....2,100 / 4,200
Standard Deduction $ (single / joint) .... 5,450 / 10,900
Federal Income Tax Paid - Deduction Allowed .... Limits
Up to $5,000.

Social Security Income - Tax Exempt .... Limits
65% for 2010; 80% in 2011; and 100% for 2012 and thereafter.

Retired Military Pay - Tax Exempt .... Limits
State & Local Government Pensions - Tax Exempt .. Limits
Federal Civil Service Pensions - Tax Exempt .... Limits
Railroad Retirement - Tax Exempt ....Yes
Private Pension - Tax Exempt .... Limits

Note: Limits include exemptions based on age, income, and other variables.

VEHICLES

Registration Fees .... 1 Year
Registration fees for passenger vehicles are determined by your vehicle's taxable horsepower.
Under 12 horsepower, $21.75.
12 - 71 horsepower, $24.75 - $48.75.
72 or more horsepower, $54.75.

Annual Vehicle Tax ....Yes
Annual property tax on vehicles.

State Emissions Test Required ....Yes
Every two years. Only in St. Louis, St. Charles, Franklin, and Jefferson counties, and the City of St. Louis. Motor vehicles and RV's with GVWR over 8,500 lbs are exempt. Web Site: www.dnr.mo.gov/gatewayvip.

Vehicle Safety Inspection Required ....Yes
Every two years. Vehicles 5 years old or less are exempt.

Mandatory Minimum Liability Insurance 25/50/10
Uninsured Motorist coverage is also required.

COST OF LIVING INDICATORS

Rank: 1 highest; 51 lowest

Cost of Living - average statewide (rank) 44
Per Capita Income (rank / $) .... 36 / 35,228
Median Household Income (rank / $) .... 36 / 46,847
Median House Value (rank / $) ....35 / 137,100
Median Property Tax on Homes (rank) 36
Fuel - avg per gal $, Mar 2010 (diesel / gas) .....2.68 / 2.51
Fuel Taxes - per gallon $ (diesel / gas) ....0.417 / 0.357
Cigarette Tax - pack of 20 ($) 1.18
Tax Burden - average all taxes (rank) 33

STATE & LOCAL REVENUE SOURCES

Rank: 1 highest; 51 lowest
Rank and % of total revenue from:

Tax Revenue (see "Details" listed below) ....36 / 38.56
Charges & Misc. Revenue .... 30 / 19.52
Federal Government ....20 / 17.38
Utility Revenue ....24 / 03.42
Insurance Trust Revenue ....07 / 21.12

Tax Revenue Details (rank / %)

Property Tax..30 / 27.40
Sales & Gross Receipts ....18 / 37.59
Individual Income Tax......................................16 / 26.93
Corporate Income Tax......................................44 / 02.04
Motor Vehicle License......................................33 / 01.38
Other Taxes...31 / 04.66

POPULATION

Rank: 1 highest; 51 lowest

State Population (rank / count) ....18 / 5,987,580
Population Per Square Mile (rank / count) .... 28 / 86

VOTING

Registration Requirements: In-person registration deadline is 28 days before election.

Address Requirements: Physical/street address required.

Register by Mail: Yes, registration deadline is 28 days before election.

Absentee Voting: Yes, excuse required.

Web Site: www.sos.mo.gov/elections/

RESOURCES

Missouri State Government
Phone: 573-751-2000
Web Site: www.missouri.gov

Missouri Department of Revenue
Phone: 573-751-4450
Web Site: www.dor.mo.gov

Missouri Motor Vehicle Department
Phone: 573-751-4509
Web Site: www.dor.mo.gov/mvdl

Missouri Office of Tourism
Phone: 800-519-2100
Web Site: www.visitmo.com

Montana

WEATHER

	Billings			Great Falls		
	🌡	💧	❄	🌡	💧	❄
Jan	32/14	0.8	9.1	31/12	0.9	9.9
Feb	38/19	0.6	7.8	37/17	0.6	8.3
Mar	45/25	1.1	10.1	43/22	1	10.4
Apr	57/34	1.8	7.9	55/32	1.4	7.2
May	67/44	2.4	1.5	65/41	2.5	1.8
Jun	77/52	2.1	0	74/49	2.6	0.3
Jul	86/58	1.1	0	83/54	1.4	0
Aug	85/57	0.9	0	81/53	1.5	0.1
Sep	72/47	1.3	1.1	70/44	1.1	1.5
Oct	61/37	1.1	3.7	59/36	0.8	3.4
Nov	45/26	0.8	6.8	44/25	0.7	7.5
Dec	36/18	0.7	8.5	35/16	0.7	8.7
🌡	Average monthly high and low temperatures in degrees Fahrenheit.					
💧	Average monthly precipitation totals in inches.					
❄	Average monthly snowfall totals in inches.					

STATE AND LOCAL TAXES

State Sales Tax (%) .... None
Local Sales Taxes (up to an additional %) .... None
Inheritance Tax .... No
Estate Tax.. No

PERSONAL INCOME TAXES

State Income Tax (%) .... 1 - 6.9
7 income brackets - Lowest $2,600; Highest $15,600.

Personal Exemption $ (single / joint) ....2,140 / 4,280
Additional $2,040 if age 65 or over.

Standard Deduction $ (single / joint)......................See note
$1,780 to $4,010 for single filers and $3,560 to $8,020 for joint returns, depending on adjusted gross income.

Federal Income Tax Paid - Deduction Allowed ....See note
Available only if you are itemizing deductions.

Social Security Income - Tax Exempt............................ Limits

Retired Military Pay - Tax Exempt ....Limits
State & Local Government Pensions - Tax Exempt ..Limits
Federal Civil Service Pensions - Tax Exempt ....Limits
Railroad Retirement - Tax Exempt ....Yes
Private Pension - Tax Exempt ....Limits

Note: Limits include a maximum combined exemption of $3,600 (adjusted annually for inflation) from all retirement income sources for taxpayers with an adjusted gross income of less than $30,000. Social Security benefits are taxed if income exceeds $25,000 (including Social Security income).

VEHICLES

Registration Fees .... 1 Year
Passenger car, pickup truck 1-ton and under, van and SUV rate is based on the age of the vehicle:
0 - 4 years old, $217.
5 - 10 years old, $87.
11 years or more, $28.
You can choose 1 or 2 year renewal periods. For vehicles 11 years old or older you can also choose to permanently register the vehicle for a registration rate of $87.50.

Motor home:
Less than 2 years old, $282.50.
2 - 4 years old, $224.25.
5 - 7 years old, $132.50.
8 years or more, $97.50.
For motor homes 11 years old or older you can choose the permanent registration option for $237.50.
Motor homes must also pay a $5 fee for Montana Highway Patrol Salary and Retention Fee and a $5 New Issue Plate Fee.

Travel Trailer:
All travel trailers must be permanently registered. The one time fee varies by length of trailer. Under 16 feet, $72. 16-feet and over, $152.
Trailer registration will also include a $5 fee for Montana Highway Patrol Salary and Retention Fee and a $5 New Issue Plate Fee.

Annual Vehicle Tax ....Yes
An annual "County Option Tax" imposed by most counties is due with the registration fee.

State Emissions Test Required ....No
Vehicle Safety Inspection Required ....No
Mandatory Minimum Liability Insurance 25/50/10

COST OF LIVING INDICATORS

Rank: 1 highest; 51 lowest

Cost of Living - average statewide (rank) 19
Per Capita Income (rank / $) .... 39 / 34,256
Median Household Income (rank / $) ....42 / 43,948
Median House Value (rank / $).........................28 / 168,200
Median Property Tax on Homes (rank) 30
Fuel - avg per gal $, Mar 2010 (diesel / gas) .....2.89 / 2.70
Fuel Taxes - per gallon $ (diesel / gas)............0.530 / 0.462
Cigarette Tax - pack of 20 ($) 2.71
Tax Burden - average all taxes (rank) 41

STATE & LOCAL REVENUE SOURCES

Rank: 1 highest; 51 lowest
Rank and % of total revenue from:

Tax Revenue (see "Details" listed below) ....43 / 35.62
Charges & Misc. Revenue...24 / 20.85
Federal Government ....07 / 21.96
Utility Revenue...46 / 01.18
Insurance Trust Revenue...10 / 20.40

Tax Revenue Details (rank / %)

Property Tax..15 / 33.83
Sales & Gross Receipts ....47 / 16.36
Individual Income Tax...19 / 25.46
Corporate Income Tax...13 / 05.46
Motor Vehicle License...02 / 04.77
Other Taxes ....06 / 14.12

POPULATION

Rank: 1 highest; 51 lowest

State Population (rank / count) ....44 / 974,989
Population Per Square Mile (rank / count) ....49 / 7

VOTING

Registration Requirements: In-person registration deadline is the day of election.

Address Requirements: Physical/street address required.

Register by Mail: Yes, registration deadline is 30 days before election.

Absentee Voting: Yes, no excuse is required.

Web Site: http://sos.mt.gov/elb/Voter_Information.asp

RESOURCES

Montana State Government
Phone: 406-444-2511
Web Site: www.mt.gov

Montana Department of Revenue
Phone: 406-444-6900
Web Site: www.mt.gov/revenue

Montana Driver Services
Phone: 406-846-6000
Web Site: www.doj.mt.gov/driving

Montana Office of Tourism
Phone: 800-847-4868
Web Site: www.visitmt.com

Nebraska

WEATHER

	Omaha			Sidney		
	🌡	💧	❄	🌡	💧	❄
Jan	31/11	0.8	7.4	38/11	0.4	6.4
Feb	37/17	0.9	6.6	42/15	0.4	5
Mar	48/27	1.9	6.4	46/19	1	8.5
Apr	63/40	2.8	1	58/29	1.6	5.9
May	74/51	4.3	0.1	69/41	3	1.4
Jun	84/61	4.1	0	81/51	3.2	0
Jul	88/66	3.8	0	88/56	2.7	0
Aug	86/64	3.8	0	87/55	1.9	0
Sep	77/54	3.4	0	78/45	1.4	0.1
Oct	66/42	2.1	0.3	65/33	0.9	2
Nov	49/29	1.5	2.6	49/20	0.6	6.4
Dec	36/17	0.9	5.5	42/15	0.4	5

🌡	Average monthly high and low temperatures in degrees Fahrenheit.
💧	Average monthly precipitation totals in inches.
❄	Average monthly snowfall totals in inches.

STATE AND LOCAL TAXES

State Sales Tax (%) 5.50
　　　Exempt: food and prescription drugs.

Local Sales Taxes (up to an additional %) 1.50
Inheritance Tax ....Yes
Estate Tax... No

PERSONAL INCOME TAXES

State Income Tax (%) ....2.56 - 6.84
　　　4 income brackets - Lowest $2,400; Highest $27,000.

Personal Exemption $ (single / joint) ....118 / 236
　　　Amount is a tax credit.

Standard Deduction $ (single / joint).........5,700 / 11,400
Federal Income Tax Paid - Deduction Allowed .... None
Social Security Income - Tax Exempt........................... Limits
　　　Taxable to the extent of federal taxation.

Retired Military Pay - Tax Exempt .... No
State & Local Government Pensions - Tax Exempt .... No

Federal Civil Service Pensions - Tax Exempt .... No
Railroad Retirement - Tax Exempt .... Yes
Private Pension - Tax Exempt .... No

VEHICLES

Registration Fees .... 1 Year
> *Motor vehicles are titled and registered at the county level in Nebraska. Annual fees are determined by the make and model of the vehicle, as well as the county. You will need to contact the County Treasurer's Office for specific fees and taxes.*

> *You can obtain an estimate by entering the required information in the "Motor Vehicle Tax Estimator" at www.nebraska.gov/dmv_cgi/vte/cgi/dmv.cgi. Along with the vehicle information you will need to know the city and county name.*

Annual Vehicle Tax ....Yes
> *All fees are included in the registration process.*

State Emissions Test Required .... No
Vehicle Safety Inspection Required .... No
Mandatory Minimum Liability Insurance 25/50/25

COST OF LIVING INDICATORS
> *Rank: 1 highest; 51 lowest*

Cost of Living - average statewide (rank) 48
Per Capita Income (rank / $) .... 26 / 37,730
Median Household Income (rank / $) .... 29 / 49,731
Median House Value (rank / $).........................40 / 122,500
Median Property Tax on Homes (rank) 18
Fuel - avg per gal $, Mar 2010 (diesel / gas).....2.82 / 2.74
Fuel Taxes - per gallon $ (diesel / gas)...........0.512 / 0.452
Cigarette Tax - pack of 20 ($) 1.65
Tax Burden - average all taxes (rank)................................. 18

STATE & LOCAL REVENUE SOURCES
> *Rank: 1 highest; 51 lowest*
> *Rank and % of total revenue from:*

Tax Revenue (see "Details" listed below) ....34 / 38.63
Charges & Misc. Revenue...25 / 20.26
Federal Government ....37 / 14.66
Utility Revenue ....01 / 15.92
Insurance Trust Revenue..48 / 10.52

> *Tax Revenue Details (rank / %)*

Property Tax...16 / 33.44
Sales & Gross Receipts ....29 / 32.38
Individual Income Tax...................................29 / 23.12

Corporate Income Tax..36 / 02.98
Motor Vehicle License..19 / 01.82
Other Taxes ....23 / 06.26

POPULATION
> *Rank: 1 highest; 51 lowest*

State Population (rank / count) .... 38 / 1,796,619
Population Per Square Mile (rank / count) .... 44 / 23

VOTING

Registration Requirements: In-person registration deadline is the second Friday before election.

Address Requirements: Physical/street address required.

Register by Mail: Yes, registration deadline is the third Friday before election.

Absentee Voting: Yes, no excuse is required.

Web Site: www.sos.ne.gov/elec/2008/index.html

RESOURCES

Nebraska State Government
Phone: 402-471-2311
Web Site: www.nebraska.gov

Nebraska Department of Revenue
Phone: 402-471-5729
Web Site: www.revenue.state.ne.us

Nebraska Department of Motor Vehicles
Phone: 402-471-3918
Web Site: www.dmv.state.ne.us

Nebraska Office of Tourism
Phone: 877-632-7275
Web Site: www.visitnebraska.org

Nevada

WEATHER

	Las Vegas			Reno		
	🌡	💧	❄	🌡	💧	❄
Jan	56/34	0.6	1	45/19	1	6
Feb	63/38	0.5	0.1	51/24	0.9	5.2
Mar	69/44	0.5	0	56/27	0.8	4.4
Apr	78/51	0.2	0	64/31	0.4	1.2
May	88/60	0.2	0	72/38	0.7	0.9
Jun	99/69	0.1	0	82/44	0.4	0
Jul	104/76	0.4	0	91/49	0.3	0
Aug	102/74	0.5	0	89/47	0.2	0
Sep	94/66	0.3	0	81/41	0.3	0
Oct	81/54	0.2	0	70/32	0.4	0.3
Nov	66/42	0.4	0.1	55/25	0.8	2.2
Dec	57/34	0.4	0.1	46/20	1	4.4

🌡	Average monthly high and low temperatures in degrees Fahrenheit.
💧	Average monthly precipitation totals in inches.
❄	Average monthly snowfall totals in inches.

STATE AND LOCAL TAXES

State Sales Tax (%) 6.85
    Exempt: food and prescription drugs.

Local Sales Taxes (up to an additional %) 0.875
Inheritance Tax .... No
Estate Tax..Yes
    Limited to federal estate tax collection.

PERSONAL INCOME TAXES

State Income Tax (%) .... None
Personal Exemption $ (single / joint) .... n/a
Standard Deduction $ (single / joint)............................. n/a
Federal Income Tax Paid - Deduction Allowed .... n/a
Social Security Income - Tax Exempt.......................... n/a
Retired Military Pay - Tax Exempt .... n/a
State & Local Government Pensions - Tax Exempt .... n/a
Federal Civil Service Pensions - Tax Exempt .... n/a
Railroad Retirement - Tax Exempt .... n/a
Private Pension - Tax Exempt .... n/a

VEHICLES

Registration Fees .... 1 Year
    Nevada charges a basic Registration Fee, Governmental Services Taxes, and other miscellaneous fees.

    Basic registration fee is $33 for passenger cars, trucks and motorcycles under 6,000 lbs. There are graduated scales based on weight for larger vehicles.

    The "Governmental Services Tax" is based on a percentage of the vehicles value. The counties of Clark and Churchill also have a "Supplemental Government Services Tax".

    The Governmental Services Tax is 4 cents on each $1.00 of the depreciated DMV Valuation (35% of the original MSRP) of the vehicle. The DMV Valuation is depreciated 5% after the first year and 10% per year thereafter until it reaches a minimum of 15%. The minimum Governmental Services Tax is $16.

    Supplemental Governmental Services Tax is 1 cent on each $1.00 of the depreciated DMV Valuation.

    You can estimate your total registration cost online at https://dmvapp.state.nv.us/VR_Estimate/VREstimationInput.aspx. You will need to know the county and vehicle information.

Annual Vehicle Tax ....Yes
    All fees are included in the registration process.

State Emissions Test Required ....Yes
    Annual. Only in the urban areas of Clark and Washoe counties. Diesel powered vehicles over 14,000 lbs GVWR are exempt. Web Site: www.dmvnv.com/emission.htm.

Vehicle Safety Inspection Required .... No
Mandatory Minimum Liability Insurance 15/30/10

COST OF LIVING INDICATORS

    Rank: 1 highest; 51 lowest

Cost of Living - average statewide (rank) 15
Per Capita Income (rank / $) ....19 / 40,353
Median Household Income (rank / $) ....16 / 56,432
Median House Value (rank / $).........................09 / 296,200
Median Property Tax on Homes (rank) 25
Fuel - avg per gal $, Mar 2010 (diesel / gas) .....2.88 / 2.79
Fuel Taxes - per gallon $ (diesel / gas)...........0.522 / 0.422
    Local taxes can add up to 9 cents on gasoline.

Cigarette Tax - pack of 20 ($) 1.81
Tax Burden - average all taxes (rank) 50

STATE & LOCAL REVENUE SOURCES

Rank: 1 highest; 51 lowest

Rank and % of total revenue from:

Tax Revenue (see "Details" listed below) ....15 / 45.00
Charges & Misc. Revenue..21 / 21.22
Federal Government ....50 / 10.65
Utility Revenue..19 / 04.28
Insurance Trust Revenue...18 / 18.85

Tax Revenue Details (rank / %)

Property Tax..29 / 27.53
Sales & Gross Receipts ....02 / 58.19
Individual Income Tax..44 / 0
Corporate Income Tax...46 / 0
Motor Vehicle License...24 / 01.63
Other Taxes ....08 / 12.65

POPULATION

Rank: 1 highest; 51 lowest

State Population (rank / count) ....35 / 2,643,085
Population Per Square Mile (rank / count) .... 43 / 24

VOTING

Registration Requirements: In-person registration deadline is 15 days before election.

Address Requirements: Physical/street address required.

Register by Mail: Yes, registration deadline is the third Friday before election.

Absentee Voting: Yes, no excuse is required.

Web Site: http://sos.state.nv.us/elections/

RESOURCES

Nevada State Government
Phone: 775-687-5000
Web Site: www.nv.gov

Nevada Department of Taxation
Phone: 775-684-2000
Web Site: www.tax.state.nv.us

Nevada Department of Motor Vehicles
Phone: 877-368-7828
Web Site: www.dmvnv.com

Nevada Office of Tourism
Phone: 800-638-2328
Web Site: www.travelnevada.com

New Hampshire

WEATHER

	Berlin			Concord		
	🌡	💧	❄	🌡	💧	❄
Jan	28/2	2.9	22.8	31/9	2.7	17.7
Feb	30/4	2.6	22.7	34/11	2.4	14.6
Mar	38/16	3.2	20.8	43/22	2.9	10.9
Apr	51/29	2.8	6.6	57/32	3	2.4
May	65/39	3.1	0.4	69/42	3.1	0.1
Jun	74/48	3.8	0	78/52	3	0
Jul	79/54	3.6	0	83/57	3.1	0
Aug	77/51	2.3	0	80/55	3.3	0
Sep	69/44	3.5	0	72/46	3	0
Oct	57/35	3.1	1	61/35	3.2	0.1
Nov	43/24	3.5	9.7	48/28	3.8	3.8
Dec	30/9	3	17.9	35/15	3.2	13.6
🌡	Average monthly high and low temperatures in degrees Fahrenheit.					
💧	Average monthly precipitation totals in inches.					
❄	Average monthly snowfall totals in inches.					

STATE AND LOCAL TAXES

State Sales Tax (%) .... None
Local Sales Taxes (up to an additional %) .... None
Inheritance Tax .... No
Estate Tax.. No

PERSONAL INCOME TAXES

State Income Tax (%) .... None
Dividends and interest income of more than $2,400 ($4,800 joint filers) subject to a 5% tax. A $1,200 exemption is available if you are age 65 or over.

Personal Exemption $ (single / joint) .... n/a
Standard Deduction $ (single / joint)............................... n/a
Federal Income Tax Paid - Deduction Allowed .... n/a
Social Security Income - Tax Exempt................................ n/a
Retired Military Pay - Tax Exempt .... n/a
State & Local Government Pensions - Tax Exempt .... n/a

Federal Civil Service Pensions - Tax Exempt .... n/a
Railroad Retirement - Tax Exempt .... n/a
Private Pension - Tax Exempt .... n/a

VEHICLES

Registration Fees .... 1 Year
State registration fees are calculated based on vehicle weight.
0 - 3,000 lbs, $61.20.
3,001 - 5,000 lbs, 7$3.20.
5,001 - 8,000 lbs, $100.20.
8,001 - 73,280 lbs, $0.96 per hundred pounds gross weight plus $45 to $75 in additional surcharges, based on weight.

In addition to the state rates, local fees are calculated as follows: Current year vehicles are taxed at $18 per $1,000 vehicle value (MSRP when new) for the first year. The rate is then reduced by $3 per $1,000 value per year until the vehicle is six years old. At that time, the rate remains at $3 per $1,000 value.

Annual Vehicle Tax ....Yes
All fees are included in the registration process.

State Emissions Test Required ....Yes
Statewide, part of annual vehicle safety inspection. Required for all 1996 and newer light-duty (8,500 GVWR and less) gasoline-fueled and 1997 and newer diesel powered passenger vehicles. Web Site: www.nh.gov/safety/divisions/dmv/emissions/index.html.

Vehicle Safety Inspection Required ....Yes
Annual. All vehicles.

Mandatory Minimum Liability Insurance 25/50/25
Amounts shown are the recommended minimum. No mandatory minimum liability requirements, except for high risk drivers. Uninsured Motorist coverage is required as well as a mandatory $1,000 medical payments coverage.

COST OF LIVING INDICATORS

Rank: 1 highest; 51 lowest

Cost of Living - average statewide (rank) 12
Per Capita Income (rank / $) .... 10 / 42830
Median Household Income (rank / $) ....07 / 63,235
Median House Value (rank / $) ....12 / 260,300
Median Property Tax on Homes (rank) 03
Fuel - avg per gal $, Mar 2010 (diesel / gas) .....2.87 / 2.64
Fuel Taxes - per gallon $ (diesel / gas)...........0.440 / 0.380

Cigarette Tax - pack of 20 ($) 2.79
Tax Burden - average all taxes (rank) 47

STATE & LOCAL REVENUE SOURCES

Rank: 1 highest; 51 lowest
Rank and % of total revenue from:

Tax Revenue (see "Details" listed below) ....10 / 45.75
Charges & Misc. Revenue...08 / 24.71
Federal Government ....27 / 16.25
Utility Revenue ....48 / 00.87
Insurance Trust Revenue..43 / 12.42

Tax Revenue Details (rank / %)

Property Tax..01 / 61.39
Sales & Gross Receipts ....48 / 15.50
Individual Income Tax..42 / 02.27
Corporate Income Tax...02 / 12.56
Motor Vehicle License..20 / 01.81
Other Taxes ....22 / 06.47

POPULATION

Rank: 1 highest; 51 lowest

State Population (rank / count) ....40 / 1,324,575
Population Per Square Mile (rank / count) ....19 / 142

VOTING

Registration Requirements: In-person registration deadline is the day of election.

Address Requirements: Physical/street address required.

Register by Mail: No

Absentee Voting: Yes, excuse required.

Web Site: www.sos.nh.gov/electionsnew.htm

RESOURCES

New Hampshire State Government
Phone: 603-271-1110
Web Site: www.nh.gov

New Hampshire Department of Revenue Administration
Phone: 603-271-2191
Web Site: www.nh.gov/revenue

New Hampshire Division of Motor Vehicles
Phone: 603-271-2251
Web Site: www.nh.gov/safety/divisions/dmv

New Hampshire Office of Tourism
Phone: 800-386-4664
Web Site: www.visitnh.gov

New Jersey

WEATHER

	Atlantic City			Newark		
	🌡	💧	❄	🌡	💧	❄
Jan	41/22	3.3	5.2	38/24	3.4	7.5
Feb	43/24	2.9	5.4	41/25	3	7.9
Mar	51/31	3.9	2.6	50/33	4	4.9
Apr	61/40	3.3	0.3	61/43	3.7	0.7
May	71/50	3.3	0	72/53	3.9	0
Jun	80/59	2.5	0	81/62	3.3	0
Jul	85/65	4.3	0	86/68	4.2	0
Aug	83/64	4.3	0	84/67	4.1	0
Sep	77/56	3	0	77/59	3.6	0
Oct	66/44	2.9	0	66/48	3	0
Nov	56/36	3.3	0.4	54/39	3.8	0.5
Dec	45/26	3.2	2.2	42/28	3.4	5.5
🌡	Average monthly high and low temperatures in degrees Fahrenheit.					
💧	Average monthly precipitation totals in inches.					
❄	Average monthly snowfall totals in inches.					

STATE AND LOCAL TAXES

State Sales Tax (%) 7.00
   Exempt: food and prescription drugs.

Local Sales Taxes (up to an additional %) ....See note
   Local sales tax on some items sold in Atlantic City and
   Cape May County.

Inheritance Tax ....Yes
   Some beneficiaries are exempt from the tax.

Estate Tax..Yes

PERSONAL INCOME TAXES

State Income Tax (%) ....1.4 - 8.9
   6 income brackets - Lowest $20,000; Highest $500,000.
   City and/or county income taxes not included.

Personal Exemption $ (single / joint) ....1,000 / 2,000
   Additional $1,000 if age 65 or over.

Standard Deduction $ (single / joint)..........................None

Federal Income Tax Paid - Deduction Allowed .... None
Social Security Income - Tax Exempt ....Yes
Retired Military Pay - Tax Exempt ....Yes
State & Local Government Pensions - Tax Exempt .. Limits
Federal Civil Service Pensions - Tax Exempt .... Limits
Railroad Retirement - Tax Exempt ....Yes
Private Pension - Tax Exempt .... Limits

Note: Limits include a maximum combined exemption of $15,000 (if 62 or older), income limits apply, from all retirement income sources.

VEHICLES

Registration Fees .... 1 Year
Registration fees are based on the vehicle weight and model year. Following are the vehicle age groups, your actual rate will vary by weight.
1970 or older, $35.50 - $65.50.
1971 - 1979, $38.50 - $72.50.
1980 - 2006, $46.50 - $71.50.
2007 - 2010, $59 - 84.

Motor homes and station wagons, fee based upon the vehicle's passenger weight class and model year. Use the highest dollar amount shown above for the year range.

Non-commercial trucks (pick-up truck, van and SUVs), fee based on the vehicle's gross weight.

New Jersey requires payment for a four-year registration period on purchases of new vehicles. They offer a rate calculator at: www.state.nj.us/mvc/regfee/index.html.

Annual Vehicle Tax .... No
No property tax on vehicles.

State Emissions Test Required ....Yes
Every 2 years. Also includes the vehicle safety inspection. Diesel-powered motor homes and recreational vehicles 18,000 lbs GVWR or more must also be tested
Web Site: www.state.nj.us/mvc/Inspections/index.htm

Vehicle Safety Inspection Required ....Yes
Every 2 years.

Mandatory Minimum Liability Insurance 15/30/5
Amounts shown are for a "Standard Policy". Other options are available. Personal Injury Protection, Uninsured and Underinsured Motorists coverage is also required. Samples of a Basic Policy and a Standard Policy are available at www.state.nj.us/dobi/division_ consumers/insurance/basicpolicy.shtml.

COST OF LIVING INDICATORS

Rank: 1 highest; 51 lowest

Cost of Living - average statewide (rank) 05
Per Capita Income (rank / $) .... 03 / 50,919
Median Household Income (rank / $) .... 02 / 70,347
Median House Value (rank / $) .... 04 / 367,600
Median Property Tax on Homes (rank) 01
Fuel - avg per gal $, Mar 2010 (diesel / gas) .....2.80 / 2.56
Fuel Taxes - per gallon $ (diesel / gas)...........0.419 / 0.329
Cigarette Tax - pack of 20 ($) 3.71
Tax Burden - average all taxes (rank) 01

STATE & LOCAL REVENUE SOURCES

Rank: 1 highest; 51 lowest
Rank and % of total revenue from:

Tax Revenue (see "Details" listed below) ....02 / 53.98
Charges & Misc. Revenue..47 / 16.17
Federal Government ....45 / 12.36
Utility Revenue ....41 / 01.75
Insurance Trust Revenue..31 / 15.74

Tax Revenue Details (rank / %)

Property Tax..03 / 41.77
Sales & Gross Receipts ....43 / 23.89
Individual Income Tax...30 / 22.80
Corporate Income Tax...12 / 05.61
Motor Vehicle License...41 / 00.87
Other Taxes ....29 / 05.06

POPULATION

Rank: 1 highest; 51 lowest

State Population (rank / count) .... 11 / 8,707,739
Population Per Square Mile (rank / count) ....02 / 998

VOTING

Registration Requirements: In-person registration deadline is 21 days before election.

Address Requirements: Physical/street address required.

Register by Mail: Yes, registration deadline is 21 days before election.

Absentee Voting: Yes, no excuse is required.

Web Site: www.njelections.org/

RESOURCES

New Jersey State Government
Phone: 609-292-2121
Web Site: www.state.nj.us

New Jersey Division of the Treasury
Phone: 609-292-6400
Web Site: www.state.nj.us/treasury/taxation

New Jersey Motor Vehicle Commission
Phone: 609-292-6500
Web Site: www.state.nj.us/mvc

New Jersey Office of Tourism
Phone: 800-847-4865
Web Site: www.visitnj.org

New Mexico

WEATHER

	Albuquerque			Las Cruces		
	🌡	💧	❄	🌡	💧	❄
Jan	47/23	0.4	2.5	56/36	0.7	1.4
Feb	53/27	0.4	2.2	59/37	0.6	1.6
Mar	61/33	0.5	1.8	66/44	0.7	0.8
Apr	71/41	0.4	0.6	75/53	0.3	0
May	80/50	0.6	0	83/60	0.3	0
Jun	90/60	0.5	0	94/70	0.5	0
Jul	92/65	1.3	0	93/70	1.8	0
Aug	89/63	1.5	0	92/70	1.7	0
Sep	83/56	0.9	0	87/64	0.8	0
Oct	72/44	0.9	0.1	76/54	1.2	0
Nov	57/32	0.5	1.3	65/41	0.1	0.2
Dec	48/24	0.5	2.6	57/35	0.7	3.9

🌡	Average monthly high and low temperatures in degrees Fahrenheit.
💧	Average monthly precipitation totals in inches.
❄	Average monthly snowfall totals in inches.

STATE AND LOCAL TAXES

State Sales Tax (%)..See note
New Mexico has a gross receipts tax with a minimum of 5.375%. Rate varies by municipality. Exempt: prescription drugs.

Local Sales Taxes (up to an additional %) 2.68
Inheritance Tax .... No
Estate Tax...Yes
Limited to federal estate tax collection.

PERSONAL INCOME TAXES

State Income Tax (%) ....1.7 - 5.3
4 income brackets - Lowest $5,500; Highest $16,000.

Personal Exemption $ (single / joint) ....3,500 / 7,000
Additional deduction up to $10,900 if age 65 or over.

Standard Deduction $ (single / joint).........5,450 / 10,900
Federal Income Tax Paid - Deduction Allowed ....None
Social Security Income - Tax Exempt...........................Limits

Retired Military Pay - Tax Exempt .... Limits
State & Local Government Pensions - Tax Exempt .. Limits
Federal Civil Service Pensions - Tax Exempt .... Limits
Railroad Retirement - Tax Exempt ....Yes
Private Pension - Tax Exempt .... Limits

*Note: Limits include a maximum combined exemption
of $10,000 (if 62 or older), income limits apply, from all
retirement income sources.*

VEHICLES

Registration Fees .... 1 Year
*Basic fees, $27 - $62. Rate is determined by weight and
model year of vehicle.*

*Trucks with a declared gross vehicle weight under 26,000
lbs, $38 - $207. Rate based on weight and model year of
vehicle.*

Annual Vehicle Tax .... No
No property tax on vehicles.

State Emissions Test Required ....Yes
*Bernalillo County only. Vehicles with a GVWR of 10,001
lbs or more are exempt. Diesel vehicles are required
to pass a visible emissions test with each change of
ownership. Web Site: www.cabq.gov/aircare.*

Vehicle Safety Inspection Required .... No
Mandatory Minimum Liability Insurance 20/50/10

COST OF LIVING INDICATORS

Rank: 1 highest; 51 lowest

Cost of Living - average statewide (rank) 25
Per Capita Income (rank / $) .... 45 / 32,091
Median Household Income (rank / $) .... 43 / 43,719
Median House Value (rank / $)........................... 31 / 154,900
Median Property Tax on Homes (rank) 43
Fuel - avg per gal $, Mar 2010 (diesel / gas)......2.84 / 2.71
Fuel Taxes - per gallon $ (diesel / gas)............0.472 / 0.372
Cigarette Tax - pack of 20 ($) 1.92
Tax Burden - average all taxes (rank) 40

STATE & LOCAL REVENUE SOURCES

Rank: 1 highest; 51 lowest
Rank and % of total revenue from:

Tax Revenue (see "Details" listed below) ....44 / 35.55
Charges & Misc. Revenue...23 / 21.13
Federal Government ....08 / 21.36
Utility Revenue..35 / 02.37
Insurance Trust Revenue..15 / 19.59

Tax Revenue Details (rank / %)

Property Tax...51 / 13.54
Sales & Gross Receipts ....12 / 46.93
Individual Income Tax...40 / 15.80
Corporate Income Tax...10 / 06.17
Motor Vehicle License...07 / 02.73
Other Taxes ....05 / 14.83

POPULATION

Rank: 1 highest; 51 lowest

State Population (rank / count) .... 36 / 2,009,671
Population Per Square Mile (rank / count) .... 46 / 17

VOTING

Registration Requirements: In-person registration
deadline is 28 days before election.

Address Requirements: Physical/street address required.

Register by Mail: Yes, registration deadline is 28 days
before election.

Absentee Voting: Yes, no excuse is required.

Web Site: www.sos.state.nm.us/sos-elections.html

RESOURCES

New Mexico State Government
Phone: 505-827-9632
Web Site: www.newmexico.gov

New Mexico Taxation and Revenue Department
Phone: 505-827-0700
Web Site: www.tax.state.nm.us/trd_home.htm

New Mexico Motor Vehicle Division
Phone: 888-683-4636
Web Site: www.mvd.newmexico.gov

New Mexico Office of Tourism
Phone: 800-733-6395
Web Site: www.newmexico.org

New York

WEATHER

	New York			Rochester		
	🌡	💧	❄	🌡	💧	❄
Jan	38/26	3.5	7.5	31/17	2.2	22.7
Feb	40/27	3.1	8.4	33/17	2.2	22.4
Mar	50/35	4	5	42/25	2.5	14.4
Apr	61/44	3.8	0.9	56/36	2.7	3.6
May	72/54	4.4	0	68/46	2.7	0.3
Jun	80/63	3.6	0	78/56	2.8	0
Jul	85/69	4.4	0	82/61	2.7	0
Aug	84/67	4.1	0	80/59	3.2	0
Sep	76/60	4	0	72/51	2.8	0
Oct	65/50	3.4	0	61/42	2.6	0.2
Nov	54/41	4.4	0.9	48/33	2.9	6.7
Dec	43/31	3.8	5.4	36/23	2.5	19.6

🌡	Average monthly high and low temperatures in degrees Fahrenheit.
💧	Average monthly precipitation totals in inches.
❄	Average monthly snowfall totals in inches.

STATE AND LOCAL TAXES

State Sales Tax (%) 4.00
Exempt: food and prescription drugs.

Local Sales Taxes (up to an additional %) 5.00
Inheritance Tax .... No
Estate Tax ....Yes
On estates valued at $1 million or more with some exceptions.

PERSONAL INCOME TAXES

State Income Tax (%) ....4 - 8.97
7 income brackets - Lowest $8,000; Highest $500,000.
City and/or county income taxes not included.

Personal Exemption $ (single / joint) .... None
Standard Deduction $ (single / joint) ....7,500 / 15,000
Federal Income Tax Paid - Deduction Allowed .... None
Social Security Income - Tax Exempt ....Yes
Retired Military Pay - Tax Exempt ....Yes

State & Local Government Pensions - Tax Exempt .. Limits
Full exemption for New York state pensions. For out-of-state pensions see Private Pensions.

Federal Civil Service Pensions - Tax Exempt ....Yes
Railroad Retirement - Tax Exempt ....Yes
Private Pension - Tax Exempt ....Limits
Up to $20,000 exempt for taxpayers 59 1/2 or older.

VEHICLES

Registration Fees .... 2 Years
Registration fees for most vehicles are based on weight.
0 - 2,950 lbs, $26 - $47.
2,951 - 3,950 lbs, $48.50 - $66.50.
3,951 - 5,050 lbs, $69 - $93.
5,051 - 6,950 lbs, $95.50 - $139.
6,951 lbs or more, $140.

A Vehicle Use Tax ($10 - $80 for 2 years) is also charge in New York City and some counties.

Annual Vehicle Tax .... No
No property tax on vehicles.

State Emissions Test Required ....Yes
Annual. For model years 1996 and newer. Diesel vehicles weighing 8,500 lbs or less are exempt.
Web Site: www.nydmv.state.ny.us/vehsafe.htm

Vehicle Safety Inspection Required ....Yes
Annual. Performed with the emissions test.

Mandatory Minimum Liability Insurance 25/50/10
Additional requirements include: $50,000 per person and $100,000 per accident for death, Uninsured Motorists and basis no-fault insurance.

COST OF LIVING INDICATORS

Rank: 1 highest; 51 lowest

Cost of Living - average statewide (rank) 07
Per Capita Income (rank / $) ....07 / 48,076
Median Household Income (rank / $) ....18 / 55,980
Median House Value (rank / $)..........................07 / 311,700
Median Property Tax on Homes (rank) 04
Fuel - avg per gal $, Mar 2010 (diesel / gas).....3.12 / 2.87
Fuel Taxes - per gallon $ (diesel / gas)...........0.478 / 0.436
Local sales tax can add about 20 cents.

Cigarette Tax - pack of 20 ($) 3.76
New York City adds an additional $1.50.

Tax Burden - average all taxes (rank) 02

STATE & LOCAL REVENUE SOURCES

Rank: 1 highest; 51 lowest

Rank and % of total revenue from:

Tax Revenue (see "Details" listed below) ....09 / 45.77
Charges & Misc. Revenue.......................................49 / 14.84
Federal Government ....32 / 15.43
Utility Revenue...17 / 04.42
Insurance Trust Revenue...16 / 19.54

Tax Revenue Details (rank / %)

Property Tax...28 / 28.41
Sales & Gross Receipts ....42 / 24.26
Individual Income Tax...05 / 31.83
Corporate Income Tax...03 / 09.26
Motor Vehicle License ....42 / 00.70
Other Taxes ....26 / 5.54

POPULATION

Rank: 1 highest; 51 lowest

State Population (rank / count) ....03 / 19,541,453
Population Per Square Mile (rank / count) ....07 / 358

VOTING

Registration Requirements: In-person registration deadline is 25 days before election.

Address Requirements: Physical/street address required.

Register by Mail: Yes, registration deadline is 25 days before election.

Absentee Voting: Yes, excuse required.

Web Site: www.elections.state.ny.us/

RESOURCES

New York State Government
Phone: 518-474-8390
Web Site: www.state.ny.us

New York Department of Taxation and Finance
Phone: 518-457-5181
Web Site: www.tax.state.ny.us

New York Department of Motor Vehicles
Phone: 518-473-5595
Web Site: www.nydmv.state.ny.us

New York Office of Tourism
Phone: 800-225-5697
Web Site: www.iloveny.com

North Carolina

WEATHER

	Charlotte			Raleigh		
	🌡️	💧	❄️	🌡️	💧	❄️
Jan	51/31	3.7	2	50/30	3.5	2.2
Feb	54/33	3.7	1.7	53/31	3.5	2.6
Mar	62/40	4.6	1.2	62/38	3.7	1.3
Apr	72/49	3	0	72/47	2.8	0
May	80/58	3.6	0	79/55	3.8	0
Jun	86/65	3.5	0	85/63	3.6	0
Jul	89/69	3.8	0	89/68	4.4	0
Aug	88/68	4.1	0	87/67	4.4	0
Sep	82/62	3.3	0	81/60	3.1	0
Oct	72/50	3.2	0	72/48	3	0
Nov	62/40	3.1	0.1	62/39	2.9	0.1
Dec	53/33	3.3	0.5	53/32	3.1	0.8
🌡️	Average monthly high and low temperatures in degrees Fahrenheit.					
💧	Average monthly precipitation totals in inches.					
❄️	Average monthly snowfall totals in inches.					

STATE AND LOCAL TAXES

State Sales Tax (%) 5.75
Exempt: food and prescription drugs. A 3% Highway Use Tax is charged on vehicle purchases in lieu of a sales tax.

Local Sales Taxes (up to an additional %) 2.50
Food and prescription drugs subject to a 2% county tax.

Inheritance Tax .... No
Estate Tax...Yes
Limited to federal estate tax collection.

PERSONAL INCOME TAXES

State Income Tax (%) ....6 - 7.75
3 income brackets - Lowest $12,750; Highest $60,000.

Personal Exemption $ (single / joint) ....1,000 / 2,000
Taxpayers who claim deductions on their federal return must make adjustments based on income level.

Standard Deduction $ (single / joint)............3,000 / 6,000
Federal Income Tax Paid - Deduction Allowed .... None
Social Security Income - Tax Exempt...................Yes
Retired Military Pay - Tax Exempt .... Limits
State & Local Government Pensions - Tax Exempt .. Limits
Federal Civil Service Pensions - Tax Exempt .... Limits
Railroad Retirement - Tax Exempt ....Yes
Private Pension - Tax Exempt .... Limits

Note: Limits include a maximum combined exemption of $4,000 (full exemption on some pensions depending on dates and length of service) from all retirement income sources. Up to $2,000 on qualifying private pensions.

VEHICLES

Registration Fees .... 1 Year
Passenger vehicles $28.

Private trucks 4,000 - 6,000 lbs, $28 - $51.60.

House trailer and/or camping trailer, $11.

A 3% Highway Use Tax is charged every time a vehicle title is transferred, based on the vehicle value. Vehicles already titled in your name from another state 90 days prior to registering in North Carolina will be taxed, maximum of $150. If owned less than 90 days a tax credit will be allowed for the amount paid to the other state. If the vehicle was titled after 90 days of purchase from a dealer, no credit will be allowed.

Annual Vehicle Tax ....Yes
Annual property tax on vehicles. Varies by county.

State Emissions Test Required ....Yes
Annual In 48 counties. Motor homes and diesel powered vehicles are exempt. Web Site: www.ncdot.org/dmv/moving/newnc/emissions.html.

Vehicle Safety Inspection Required ....Yes
Annual.

Mandatory Minimum Liability Insurance 30/60/25
Uninsured and Underinsured Motorists coverage is also required.

COST OF LIVING INDICATORS

Rank: 1 highest; 51 lowest

Cost of Living - average statewide (rank) 31
Per Capita Income (rank / $) ....37 / 46,574
Median Household Income (rank / $) ....40 / 44,441
Median House Value (rank / $)...........................33 / 145,600

Median Property Tax on Homes (rank) 39
Fuel - avg per gal $, Mar 2010 (diesel / gas).....2.85 / 2.68
Fuel Taxes - per gallon $ (diesel / gas)...........0.546 / 0.486
Cigarette Tax - pack of 20 ($) 1.46
Tax Burden - average all taxes (rank) 21

STATE & LOCAL REVENUE SOURCES

Rank: 1 highest; 51 lowest
Rank and % of total revenue from:

Tax Revenue (see "Details" listed below) ....20 / 42.72
Charges & Misc. Revenue..20 / 21.24
Federal Government ....15 / 18.79
Utility Revenue ....16 / 04.63
Insurance Trust Revenue..42 / 12.62

Tax Revenue Details (rank / %)

Property Tax...41 / 22.54
Sales & Gross Receipts ....26 / 34.01
Individual Income Tax...04 / 32.66
Corporate Income Tax...17 / 04.83
Motor Vehicle License ....18 / 02.00
Other Taxes ....37 / 03.96

POPULATION

Rank: 1 highest; 51 lowest

State Population (rank / count) ....10 / 9,380,884
Population Per Square Mile (rank / count) ....16 / 174

VOTING

Registration Requirements: In-person registration deadline is 25 days before election.

Address Requirements: Physical/street address required.

Register by Mail: Yes, registration deadline is 25 days before election.

Absentee Voting: Yes, no excuse is required.

Web Site: www.sboe.state.nc.us/

RESOURCES

North Carolina State Government
Phone: 919-733-1110
Web Site: www.ncgov.com

North Carolina Department of Revenue
Phone: 877-252-3052
Web Site: www.dor.state.nc.us

North Carolina Division of Motor Vehicles
Phone: 919-715-7000
Web Site: www.ncdot.org/dmv

North Carolina Office of Tourism
Phone: 800-847-4862
Web Site: www.visitnc.com

North Dakota

WEATHER

	Bismarck			Fargo		
	🌡	💧	❄	🌡	💧	❄
Jan	19/-1	0.5	7.2	15/-3	0.6	8.6
Feb	26/4	0.4	6.7	21/3	0.5	5.9
Mar	37/17	0.8	8.1	34/17	1	6.7
Apr	55/31	1.5	3.8	54/32	1.7	3.1
May	68/42	2.2	0.9	69/44	2.3	0.1
Jun	77/52	2.9	0	77/54	3.1	0
Jul	84/56	2.4	0	83/59	3.2	0
Aug	83/54	1.8	0	81/57	2.4	0
Sep	71/43	1.4	0.3	70/46	1.8	0
Oct	59/32	0.9	1.7	57/35	1.5	0.7
Nov	39/18	0.6	6.3	36/19	0.8	5.8
Dec	25/4	0.5	6.9	21/4	0.6	7.1

🌡	Average monthly high and low temperatures in degrees Fahrenheit.
💧	Average monthly precipitation totals in inches.
❄	Average monthly snowfall totals in inches.

STATE AND LOCAL TAXES

State Sales Tax (%) 5.00
Exempt: food and prescription drugs.

Local Sales Taxes (up to an additional %) 2.50
Inheritance Tax .... No
Estate Tax...Yes

PERSONAL INCOME TAXES

State Income Tax (%) .... 1.84 - 4.86
5 income brackets - Lowest $33,950; Highest $372,950.

Personal Exemption $ (single / joint) ....3,500 / 7,000
Standard Deduction $ (single / joint)......... 5,450 / 10,900
Federal Income Tax Paid - Deduction Allowed .... None
Social Security Income - Tax Exempt............................Limits
Taxable to the extent of federal taxation.

Retired Military Pay - Tax Exempt ....Limits
State & Local Government Pensions - Tax Exempt .. Limits
Federal Civil Service Pensions - Tax Exempt .... Limits

Railroad Retirement - Tax Exempt ....Yes
Private Pension - Tax Exempt .... No

*Note: Limits include a maximum combined exemption
of $5,000 from all retirement income sources including
Social Security benefits.*

VEHICLES

Registration Fees .... 1 Year
*Registration fees are based on the weight of vehicle and
the year it is first registered (model year has no bearing).
Rates below are for "Year First Registered 2003 thru
2009", rates decline as first registration year gets older.*

Passenger vehicles:
0 - 4,999 lbs, $73 - $111.
5,000 - 7,999 lbs, $142 - $208.
8,000 lbs and over, $241 - $274.

Pickup trucks:
0 - 10,000 lbs, $73 - $111.
10,001 - 16,000 lbs, $142 - $208.
16,001 lbs and over, $241 - $274.

Travel trailers, $20.

*You can estimate your vehicle registration fees online
at: https://secure.apps.state.nd.us/dot/mv/mvrenewal/
feeCalc.htm.*

Annual Vehicle Tax .... No
    No property tax on vehicles.

State Emissions Test Required .... No
Vehicle Safety Inspection Required .... No
Mandatory Minimum Liability Insurance 25/50/25
    *Personal Injury Protection, Uninsured and Underinsured
    Motorists coverage is also required.*

COST OF LIVING INDICATORS
Rank: 1 highest; 51 lowest

Cost of Living - average statewide (rank) 34
Per Capita Income (rank / $) ....21 / 39,321
Median Household Income (rank / $) ....40 / 45,996
Median House Value (rank / $)...........................47 / 106,200
Median Property Tax on Homes (rank) 26
Fuel - avg per gal $, Mar 2010 (diesel / gas) .....2.98 / 2.78
Fuel Taxes - per gallon $ (diesel / gas)...........0.474 / 0.414
Cigarette Tax - pack of 20 ($) 1.45
Tax Burden - average all taxes (rank) 34

STATE & LOCAL REVENUE SOURCES
Rank: 1 highest; 51 lowest
Rank and % of total revenue from:

Tax Revenue (see "Details" listed below) ....26 / 41.02
Charges & Misc. Revenue...14 / 22.55
Federal Government ....09 / 20.98
Utility Revenue...39 / 01.82
Insurance Trust Revenue...37 / 13.63

Tax Revenue Details (rank / %)

Property Tax...31 / 26.81
Sales & Gross Receipts ....25 / 35.12
Individual Income Tax..41 / 12.16
Corporate Income Tax..15 / 05.24
Motor Vehicle License..14 / 02.22
Other Taxes ....04 / 19.45

POPULATION
Rank: 1 highest; 51 lowest

State Population (rank / count) ....48 / 646,844
Population Per Square Mile (rank / count) ....48 / 9

VOTING

Registration Requirements: North Dakota does not have
voter registration.

Address Requirements: N/A.

Register by Mail: North Dakota does not have voter
registration.

Absentee Voting: Yes, no excuse is required.

Web Site: www.nd.gov/sos/electvote/

RESOURCES

North Dakota State Government
Phone: 701-328-2000
Web Site: www.nd.gov

North Dakota Office of State Tax Commissioner
Phone: 701-328-7088
Web Site: www.nd.gov/tax

North Dakota Motor Vehicle Division
Phone: 701-328-2500
Web Site: www.dot.nd.gov/public/licensing.htm

North Dakota Office of Tourism
Phone: 800-435-5663
Web Site: www.ndtourism.com

Ohio

WEATHER

	Cincinnati			Cleveland		
	🌡	💧	❄	🌡	💧	❄
Jan	38/21	2.5	4.9	34/19	2.6	12.6
Feb	42/24	2.5	3.9	36/21	2.3	12.3
Mar	54/34	4.2	2.6	46/28	3	10.6
Apr	65/43	3.7	0.2	58/38	3.4	2.3
May	75/52	4.4	0	69/48	3.5	0.1
Jun	83/61	3.4	0	79/58	3.5	0
Jul	86/66	4.1	0	83/62	3.6	0
Aug	85/64	3.7	0	81/61	3.4	0
Sep	78/57	3.1	0	74/54	3.2	0
Oct	67/44	2.8	0	63/44	2.6	0.6
Nov	54/35	3.3	0.7	50/35	3.2	5
Dec	43/26	3.1	1.9	38/25	2.9	11.9
🌡	Average monthly high and low temperatures in degrees Fahrenheit.					
💧	Average monthly precipitation totals in inches.					
❄	Average monthly snowfall totals in inches.					

STATE AND LOCAL TAXES

State Sales Tax (%) 5.50
  Exempt: food and prescription drugs.

Local Sales Taxes (up to an additional %) 2.00
Inheritance Tax .... No
Estate Tax...Yes

PERSONAL INCOME TAXES

State Income Tax (%) ....0.587 - 5.925
  9 income brackets - Lowest $5,000; Highest $200,000.
  City and/or county income taxes not included.

Personal Exemption $ (single / joint) ....1,500 / 3,000
Standard Deduction $ (single / joint)............................ None
Federal Income Tax Paid - Deduction Allowed .... None
Social Security Income - Tax Exempt ....Yes
Retired Military Pay - Tax Exempt ....Yes
State & Local Government Pensions - Tax Exempt .... No
Federal Civil Service Pensions - Tax Exempt .... No

Railroad Retirement - Tax Exempt ....Yes
Private Pension - Tax Exempt .... No

VEHICLES

Registration Fees .... 1 Year
  Passenger vehicles, $34.50.
  Motor home, $49.50.
  Trucks up to 3/4 ton, $49.50.
  Trucks 3/4 -1 ton, $84.50.

  A local "Permissive Tax" may be added, maximum of $20.

Annual Vehicle Tax .... No
  No property tax on vehicles.

State Emissions Test Required ....Yes
  Every two years. For Cuyahoga, Geauga, Lake, Lorain, Medina, Portage, or Summit counties. Motor homes and vehicles over 10,000 lbs are exempt.
  Web Site: www.epa..state.oh.us/dapc/mobile.aspx

Vehicle Safety Inspection Required .... No
Mandatory Minimum Liability Insurance 15.5/25/7.5

COST OF LIVING INDICATORS

  Rank: 1 highest; 51 lowest

Cost of Living - average statewide (rank) 37
Per Capita Income (rank / $) ....33 / 35,511
Median Household Income (rank / $) ....32 / 48,011
Median House Value (rank / $).........................34 / 137,800
Median Property Tax on Homes (rank) 24
Fuel - avg per gal $, Mar 2010 (diesel / gas).....2.88 / 2.59
Fuel Taxes - per gallon $ (diesel / gas)...........0.524 / 0.464
Cigarette Tax - pack of 20 ($) 2.26
  Plus 35 cents in Cuyahoga County

Tax Burden - average all taxes (rank) 07

STATE & LOCAL REVENUE SOURCES

  Rank: 1 highest; 51 lowest
  Rank and % of total revenue from:

Tax Revenue (see "Details" listed below) ....40 / 37.78
Charges & Misc. Revenue.......................................40 / 17.63
Federal Government ....35 / 14.93
Utility Revenue ....38 / 01.92
Insurance Trust Revenue..03 / 27.74

  Tax Revenue Details (rank / %)

Property Tax...26 / 28.99
Sales & Gross Receipts ....34 / 31.24
Individual Income Tax...10 / 29.85

Corporate Income Tax..41 / 02.63
Motor Vehicle License...17 / 02.12
Other Taxes ....27 / 05.17

POPULATION

Rank: 1 highest; 51 lowest

State Population (rank / count) ....07 / 11,542,645
Population Per Square Mile (rank / count) ....11 / 258

VOTING

Registration Requirements: In-person registration deadline is 30 days before election.

Address Requirements: Physical/street address required.

Register by Mail: Yes, registration deadline is 30 days before election.

Absentee Voting: Yes, no excuse is required.

Web Site: www.sos.state.oh.us/SOS/voter.aspx

RESOURCES

Ohio State Government
Phone: 614-466-2000
Web Site: www.ohio.gov

Ohio Department of Taxation
Phone: 800-282-1780
Web Site: www.tax.ohio.gov

Ohio Bureau of Motor Vehicles
Phone: 614-752-7500
Web Site: www.ohiobmv.com

Ohio Office of Tourism
Phone: 800-282-5393
Web Site: www.discoverohio.com

Oklahoma

WEATHER

	Oklahoma City			Tulsa		
	🌡	💧	❄	🌡	💧	❄
Jan	47/26	1.2	3	46/26	1.5	3.3
Feb	52/30	1.5	2.4	52/30	1.9	2.4
Mar	61/38	2.5	1.4	61/39	3.1	1.4
Apr	72/49	2.8	0	72/50	3.8	0
May	79/58	5.7	0	79/59	5.7	0
Jun	87/66	4.3	0	88/68	4.5	0
Jul	93/71	2.8	0	93/72	3.4	0
Aug	92/70	2.6	0	93/70	2.9	0
Sep	84/62	3.7	0	84/62	4.2	0
Oct	74/50	3	0	74/51	3.4	0
Nov	60/38	1.8	0.5	60/38	2.6	0.4
Dec	50/29	1.5	1.8	50/30	2	1.6
🌡	Average monthly high and low temperatures in degrees Fahrenheit.					
💧	Average monthly precipitation totals in inches.					
❄	Average monthly snowfall totals in inches.					

STATE AND LOCAL TAXES

State Sales Tax (%) 4.50
Exempt: prescription drugs.

Local Sales Taxes (up to an additional %) 7.00
Inheritance Tax .... No
Estate Tax..Yes
Estate tax is 0.5% to 10%. Additional taxes may also apply.

PERSONAL INCOME TAXES

State Income Tax (%) ....0.5 - 5.5
8 income brackets - Lowest $1,000; Highest $8,700.

Personal Exemption $ (single / joint) ....1,000 / 2,000
Additional $1,000 if age 65 or over.

Standard Deduction $ (single / joint)............4,250 / 8,500
Federal Income Tax Paid - Deduction Allowed ....Full
Social Security Income - Tax Exempt................................Yes
Retired Military Pay - Tax Exempt ....Limits

State & Local Government Pensions - Tax Exempt .. Limits
Federal Civil Service Pensions - Tax Exempt .... Limits
Railroad Retirement - Tax Exempt ....Yes
Private Pension - Tax Exempt .... Limits

> *Note: Limits include a maximum combined exemption of $10,000 (income restrictions on private pensions) from all retirement income sources other than Social Security and Railroad Retirement.*

VEHICLES

Registration Fees .... 1 Year
> *Fees are based on how long you've had the vehicle registered in the state.*
> *1st - 4th year, $91.*
> *5th - 8th year, $81.*
> *9th - 12th year, $61.*
> *13th - 16th year, $41.*
> *17th year and over, $21.*

Annual Vehicle Tax .... No
> *No property tax on vehicles.*

State Emissions Test Required .... No
Vehicle Safety Inspection Required .... No
Mandatory Minimum Liability Insurance 25/50/25

COST OF LIVING INDICATORS

> *Rank: 1 highest; 51 lowest*

Cost of Living - average statewide (rank) 51
Per Capita Income (rank / $) .... 29 / 36,899
Median Household Income (rank / $) .... 46 / 42,836
Median House Value (rank / $) .... 48 / 100,200
Median Property Tax on Homes (rank) 45
Fuel - avg per gal $, Mar 2010 (diesel / gas) .....2.67 / 2.55
Fuel Taxes - per gallon $ (diesel / gas) ....0.384 / 0.354
Cigarette Tax - pack of 20 ($) 2.04
Tax Burden - average all taxes (rank) 20

STATE & LOCAL REVENUE SOURCES

> *Rank: 1 highest; 51 lowest*
> *Rank and % of total revenue from:*

Tax Revenue (see "Details" listed below) ....33 / 39.36
Charges & Misc. Revenue..19 / 21.39
Federal Government ....16 / 18.72
Utility Revenue..14 / 04.68
Insurance Trust Revenue..30 / 15.85

> *Tax Revenue Details (rank / %)*

Property Tax...46 / 16.16

Sales & Gross Receipts ....16 / 38.11
Individual Income Tax..28 / 23.22
Corporate Income Tax...19 / 04.70
Motor Vehicle License...01 / 05.12
Other Taxes ....07 / 12.69

POPULATION

> *Rank: 1 highest; 51 lowest*

State Population (rank / count) .... 28 / 3,687,050
Population Per Square Mile (rank / count) .... 37 / 53

VOTING

Registration Requirements: In-person registration deadline is 25 days before election.

Address Requirements: Physical/street address required.

Register by Mail: Yes, registration deadline is 25 days before election.

Absentee Voting: Yes, no excuse is required.

Web Site: www.ok.gov/~elections/

RESOURCES

Oklahoma State Government
Phone: 405-521-2011
Web Site: www.ok.gov

Oklahoma Tax Commission
Phone: 405-521-3160
Web Site: www.tax.ok.gov

Oklahoma Department of Public Safety (Driver License)
Phone: 405-425-2424
Web Site: www.dps.state.ok.us

Oklahoma Motor Vehicle Division
Phone: 405-521-3279
Web Site: www.tax.ok.gov/motveh.html

Oklahoma Office of Tourism
Phone: 800-652-6552
Web Site: www.travelok.com

Oregon

WEATHER

	Eugene			Portland		
	🌡	💧	❄	🌡	💧	❄
Jan	46/33	7.9	3.7	45/34	5.4	3.3
Feb	51/35	5.5	0.8	50/36	4.1	1
Mar	56/37	5.3	0.5	56/39	3.7	0.4
Apr	61/39	3.1	0	61/42	2.5	0
May	67/43	2.3	0	68/48	2	0
Jun	74/48	1.4	0	73/53	1.6	0
Jul	82/51	0.5	0	80/57	0.5	0
Aug	82/51	0.9	0	79/57	0.9	0
Sep	77/48	1.4	0	74/52	1.6	0
Oct	64/42	3.6	0	64/46	3.1	0
Nov	53/38	7.5	0.3	52/40	5.5	0.4
Dec	47/35	8.3	1.3	46/36	6.5	1.4

🌡	Average monthly high and low temperatures in degrees Fahrenheit.
💧	Average monthly precipitation totals in inches.
❄	Average monthly snowfall totals in inches.

STATE AND LOCAL TAXES

State Sales Tax (%) .... None
Local Sales Taxes (up to an additional %) .... None
Inheritance Tax .... Yes
Some exceptions.
Estate Tax .... Yes
Some exceptions.

PERSONAL INCOME TAXES

State Income Tax (%) .... 5 - 11
5 income brackets - Lowest $3,050; Highest $250,000.
City and/or county income taxes not included.
Personal Exemption $ (single / joint) .... 169 / 338
Amount is a tax credit.
Standard Deduction $ (single / joint) .... 1,865 / 3,735
Federal Income Tax Paid - Deduction Allowed .... Limits
Up to $5,600.

Social Security Income - Tax Exempt .... Yes
Retired Military Pay - Tax Exempt .... Limits
A tax credit up to 9% is available, income limits apply. Some exceptions based on dates of service.

State & Local Government Pensions - Tax Exempt .. Limits
A tax credit up to 9% is available, income limits apply.

Federal Civil Service Pensions - Tax Exempt .... Limits
A tax credit up to 9% is available, income limits apply.

Railroad Retirement - Tax Exempt .... Yes
Private Pension - Tax Exempt .... Limits
A tax credit up to 9% is available, income limits apply.

VEHICLES

Registration Fees .... 2 Years
Passenger vehicles, $77. The very first registration period is four years (double the rate), every two years thereafter.

Camper and travel trailer, $81. Add $6.75 for each additional foot over 10 feet. (No vehicle over 45 feet can be registered.)

Motor homes 6 - 14 feet, $54.
Motor homes 15 feet, $163.50. Add $7.50 for each additional foot. (No vehicle over 45 feet can be registered.)

Annual Vehicle Tax .... No
No property tax on vehicles.

State Emissions Test Required .... Yes
Within and near the Medford or Portland-Metro areas only. Diesel powered vehicles 8,501 lbs or more are exempt. Web Site: www.deq.state.or.us/aq/vip

Vehicle Safety Inspection Required .... No
Mandatory Minimum Liability Insurance 25/50/20
Personal Injury Protection and Uninsured Motorist coverage is also required.

COST OF LIVING INDICATORS
Rank: 1 highest; 51 lowest

Cost of Living - average statewide (rank) 14
Per Capita Income (rank / $) .... 32 / 35,956
Median Household Income (rank / $) .... 27 / 50,165
Median House Value (rank / $) .... 14 / 255,300
Median Property Tax on Homes (rank) 16

Fuel - avg per gal $, Mar 2010 (diesel / gas) .....2.91 / 2.82

Fuel Taxes - per gallon $ (diesel / gas) ....0.484 / 0.424
Local taxes can add up to 5 cents on diesel and 8 cents for gas.

Cigarette Tax - pack of 20 ($) 2.19

Tax Burden - average all taxes (rank) 27

STATE & LOCAL REVENUE SOURCES

Rank: 1 highest; 51 lowest
Rank and % of total revenue from:

Tax Revenue (see "Details" listed below) ....50 / 30.54

Charges & Misc. Revenue ....22 / 21.17

Federal Government ....42 / 13.43

Utility Revenue ....27 / 03.24

Insurance Trust Revenue ....01 / 31.63

Tax Revenue Details (rank / %)

Property Tax ....19 / 31.05

Sales & Gross Receipts ....51 / 08.67

Individual Income Tax ....01 / 44.02

Corporate Income Tax ....31 / 03.63

Motor Vehicle License ....04 / 03.61

Other Taxes ....16 / 09.02

POPULATION

Rank: 1 highest; 51 lowest

State Population (rank / count) ....27 / 3,825,657

Population Per Square Mile (rank / count) .... 39 / 39

VOTING

Registration Requirements: In-person registration deadline is 21 days before election.

Address Requirements: Physical/street address required.

Register by Mail: Yes, registration deadline is 21 days before election.

Absentee Voting: Yes, no excuse is required.

Web Site: www.sos.state.or.us/elections/

RESOURCES

Oregon State Government
Phone: 503-378-6500
Web Site: www.oregon.gov

Oregon Department of Revenue
Phone: 503-378-4988
Web Site: www.oregon.gov/dor

Oregon Driver and Motor Vehicles
Phone: 503-945-5000
Web Site: www.oregon.gov/odot/dmv

Oregon Office of Tourism
Phone: 800-547-7842
Web Site: www.traveloregon.com

Pennsylvania

WEATHER

	Philadelphia			Pittsburgh		
	🌡	💧	❄	🌡	💧	❄
Jan	39/24	3.2	6.4	35/20	2.8	11.3
Feb	42/26	2.8	6.4	38/22	2.4	9.3
Mar	51/33	3.7	3.7	48/30	3.4	8.7
Apr	63/43	3.4	0.3	61/40	3.2	1.7
May	73/53	3.6	0	71/49	3.6	0.1
Jun	82/62	3.4	0	79/58	3.8	0
Jul	87/68	4.2	0	83/62	3.8	0
Aug	85/66	3.9	0	81/61	3.3	0
Sep	78/59	3.3	0	75/54	2.8	0
Oct	67/47	2.7	0	63/43	2.3	0.4
Nov	55/38	3.3	0.6	50/34	2.8	3.3
Dec	44/29	3.3	3.4	39/25	2.8	8.3

🌡	Average monthly high and low temperatures in degrees Fahrenheit.
💧	Average monthly precipitation totals in inches.
❄	Average monthly snowfall totals in inches.

STATE AND LOCAL TAXES

State Sales Tax (%) 6.00
Exempt: food and prescription drugs.

Local Sales Taxes (up to an additional %) 2.00

Inheritance Tax ....Yes
Ranges from 0% to 15% depending on value and the relationship of the recipient to the decedent.

Estate Tax ....Yes
Limited to federal estate tax collection.

PERSONAL INCOME TAXES

State Income Tax (%) 3.07
Flat rate, no income brackets. City and/or county income taxes not included.

Personal Exemption $ (single / joint) ....None
Standard Deduction $ (single / joint)............................None
Federal Income Tax Paid - Deduction Allowed ....None

Social Security Income - Tax Exempt...............................Yes
Retired Military Pay - Tax Exempt ....Yes
State & Local Government Pensions - Tax Exempt ....Yes
Federal Civil Service Pensions - Tax Exempt ....Yes
Railroad Retirement - Tax Exempt ....Yes
Private Pension - Tax Exempt ....Yes

VEHICLES

Registration Fees .... 1 Year
Passenger vehicle, $36.

Truck registration fees vary by gross weight of vehicle.
5,000 lbs or less, $58.50.
5,001 - 7,000 lbs, $81.
7,001 - 9,000 lbs, $153.
9,001 - 11,000 lbs, $198.
11,001 - 33,000 lbs, $243 - 567.
33,001 - 80,000 lbs, $621 - 1,687.50.

Motor home 8,000 lbs or less, $45.
Motor home 8,001 - 11,000 lbs, $63.
Motor home 11,000 lbs or more, $81.

Annual Vehicle Tax ....No
No property tax on vehicles.

State Emissions Test Required ....Yes
Annual. In four regions covering 25 counties.
Web Site: www.drivecleanpa.state.pa.us/drivecleanpa.

Vehicle Safety Inspection Required ....Yes
Annual.

Mandatory Minimum Liability Insurance 15/30/5
Personal Injury Protection is also required.

COST OF LIVING INDICATORS

Rank: 1 highest; 51 lowest

Cost of Living - average statewide (rank) 23
Per Capita Income (rank / $) .... 20 / 40,265
Median Household Income (rank / $) .... 25 / 50,702
Median House Value (rank / $)........................30 / 155,400
Median Property Tax on Homes (rank) 15
Fuel - avg per gal $, Mar 2010 (diesel / gas) .....3.04 / 2.76
Fuel Taxes - per gallon $ (diesel / gas)...........0.636 / 0.507
Cigarette Tax - pack of 20 ($) 2.61
Tax Burden - average all taxes (rank) 12

STATE & LOCAL REVENUE SOURCES

Rank: 1 highest; 51 lowest
Rank and % of total revenue from:

Tax Revenue (see "Details" listed below) ....18 / 43.07

Charges & Misc. Revenue...32 / 19.32
Federal Government ....30 / 15.62
Utility Revenue...36 / 02.21
Insurance Trust Revenue..13 / 19.80

Tax Revenue Details (rank / %)

Property Tax..23 / 29.59
Sales & Gross Receipts ....37 / 28.63
Individual Income Tax...19 / 25.46
Corporate Income Tax...23 / 04.38
Motor Vehicle License...27 / 01.57
Other Taxes ....11 / 10.37

POPULATION

Rank: 1 highest; 51 lowest

State Population (rank / count) ....06 / 12,604,767
Population Per Square Mile (rank / count) ....10 / 274

VOTING

Registration Requirements: In-person registration deadline is 30 days before election.

Address Requirements: Physical/street address required.

Register by Mail: Yes, registration deadline is 30 days before election.

Absentee Voting: Yes, excuse required.

Web Site: www.votespa.com/

RESOURCES

Pennsylvania State Government
Phone: 800-932-0784
Web Site: www.state.pa.us

Pennsylvania Department of Revenue
Phone: 717-787-8201
Web Site: www.revenue.state.pa.us

Pennsylvania Driver and Vehicle Services
Phone: 717-412-5300
Web Site: www.dmv.state.pa.us

Pennsylvania Office of Tourism
Phone: 800-847-4872
Web Site: www.visitpa.com

Rhode Island

WEATHER

	Newport			Providence		
	🌡	💧	❄	🌡	💧	❄
Jan	38/23	3.8	7	37/20	3.9	9.4
Feb	39/24	3.7	7	38/22	3.5	9.6
Mar	46/30	4.4	2.9	46/29	4.3	7.6
Apr	55/38	4.3	0	58/39	4.1	0.7
May	64/47	3.6	0	68/48	3.6	0.2
Jun	73/57	3	0	77/57	2.9	0
Jul	79/63	2.9	0	82/64	3.1	0
Aug	78/63	3.3	0	81/62	3.9	0
Sep	72/57	3.7	0	73/54	3.5	0
Oct	63/47	3.3	0	63/43	3.6	0.1
Nov	53/38	4.6	0.9	53/35	4.5	1
Dec	42/28	4.4	2.9	41/25	4.3	7
🌡	Average monthly high and low temperatures in degrees Fahrenheit.					
💧	Average monthly precipitation totals in inches.					
❄	Average monthly snowfall totals in inches.					

STATE AND LOCAL TAXES

State Sales Tax (%)..7.00
Exempt: food and prescription drugs.

Local Sales Taxes (up to an additional %) .... None

Inheritance Tax .... No

Estate Tax..Yes
On estates valued at $850,000 or more with some exceptions.

PERSONAL INCOME TAXES

State Income Tax (%)... 3.75 - 9.9
5 income brackets - Lowest $33,950; Highest $372,950. A flat rate tax option is also used to calculate taxes. The flat rate applies to all income with no deductions. Taxpayers pay the lesser amount. The flat rate is 6% for 2010 and 5.5% thereafter.

Personal Exemption $ (single / joint) ....3,500 / 7,000
Standard Deduction $ (single / joint)......... 5,450 / 10,900
  If age 65 or older, $6,850 for single returns and $13,200
  for married filing jointly.

Federal Income Tax Paid - Deduction Allowed .... None
Social Security Income - Tax Exempt............................Limits
  Taxed to the extent it is federally taxed.

Retired Military Pay - Tax Exempt .... No
State & Local Government Pensions - Tax Exempt .... No
Federal Civil Service Pensions - Tax Exempt .... No
Railroad Retirement - Tax Exempt ....Yes
Private Pension - Tax Exempt .... No

VEHICLES

Registration Fees .... 2 Years
  Passenger vehicles under 4,000 lbs, $61.50.
  Trucks under 4,000 lbs, $69.50.
  All Vehicles 4,000 lbs or more:
  4,001 - 7,000 lbs, $81.50 - $113.50.
  7,001 - 10,000 lbs, $129.50 - $157.50.
  10,001 - 16,000 lbs, $213.50 - $281.50.
  16,001 - 22,000 lbs, $317.50 - $389.50.
  22,001 - 30,000 lbs, $421.50 - $633.50.
  30,001 - 36,000 lbs, $845.50 - $953.50.
  36,001 - 42,000 lbs, $953.50 - $1,109.50.
  42,001 - 74,000 lbs, $1,217.50 - $1,945.50.

Annual Vehicle Tax ....Yes
  Annual property tax on vehicles, varies by municipality.

State Emissions Test Required ....Yes
  Every two years. Annual for all used vehicles over 8,500
  lbs. Web Site: www.riinspection.org

Vehicle Safety Inspection Required ....Yes
  Every 2 years. Annual for all vehicles over 8,500 lbs.

Mandatory Minimum Liability Insurance 25/50/25

COST OF LIVING INDICATORS
  Rank: 1 highest; 51 lowest

Cost of Living - average statewide (rank) 09
Per Capita Income (rank / $) .... 16 / 41,008
Median Household Income (rank / $) .... 20 / 54,562
Median House Value (rank / $)...........................11 / 290,800
Median Property Tax on Homes (rank) 05
Fuel - avg per gal $, Mar 2010 (diesel / gas).....2.98 / 2.75

Fuel Taxes - per gallon $ (diesel / gas)...........0.574 / 0.514
Cigarette Tax - pack of 20 ($) 4.47
Tax Burden - average all taxes (rank) 11

STATE & LOCAL REVENUE SOURCES
  Rank: 1 highest; 51 lowest
  Rank and % of total revenue from:

Tax Revenue (see "Details" listed below) ....21 / 42.57
Charges & Misc. Revenue..45 / 16.93
Federal Government ....17 / 18.70
Utility Revenue..42 / 01.72
Insurance Trust Revenue..11 / 20.08

  Tax Revenue Details (rank / %)

Property Tax..05 / 41.02
Sales & Gross Receipts ....38 / 28.62
Individual Income Tax...32 / 22.68
Corporate Income Tax...30 / 03.74
Motor Vehicle License ....36 / 01.10
Other Taxes ....49 / 02.84

POPULATION
  Rank: 1 highest; 51 lowest

State Population (rank / count) .... 43 / 1,053,209
Population Per Square Mile (rank / count) ....03 / 682

VOTING

Registration Requirements: In-person registration deadline is 30 days before election. Rhode Island allows Election Day registration to vote for the office of President/Vice President.

Address Requirements: Physical/street address required.

Register by Mail: Yes, registration deadline is 30 days before election.

Absentee Voting: Yes, excuse required.

Web Site: www.elections.state.ri.us/

RESOURCES

Rhode Island State Government
Phone: 401-222-2000
Web Site: www.ri.gov

Rhode Island Division of Taxation
Phone: 401-574-8829
Web Site: www.tax.ri.gov

Rhode Island Division of Motor Vehicles
Phone: 401-462-4368
Web Site: www.dmv.state.ri.us

Rhode Island Office of Tourism
Phone: 800-556-2484
Web Site: www.visitrhodeisland.com

South Carolina

WEATHER

	Charleston			Columbia		
	🌡	💧	❄	🌡	💧	❄
Jan	59/38	3.5	N/A	56/33	4.1	0.5
Feb	62/40	3.1	N/A	60/36	4	0.8
Mar	68/46	4.4	N/A	68/42	4.7	0.3
Apr	76/53	2.8	N/A	77/50	3.2	0
May	83/62	4.1	N/A	84/59	3.5	0
Jun	88/69	6	N/A	90/67	4.4	0
Jul	90/72	7.2	N/A	92/71	5.6	0
Aug	89/72	6.9	N/A	91/70	6	0
Sep	85/67	5.6	N/A	85/64	4	0
Oct	77/56	3.1	N/A	77/51	2.9	0
Nov	69/46	2.5	N/A	67/41	2.7	0
Dec	61/39	3.1	N/A	59/35	3.4	0.3

🌡	Average monthly high and low temperatures in degrees Fahrenheit.
💧	Average monthly precipitation totals in inches.
❄	Average monthly snowfall totals in inches.

STATE AND LOCAL TAXES

State Sales Tax (%) 6.00
  Exempt: food and prescription drugs.

Local Sales Taxes (up to an additional %) 2.00
Inheritance Tax .... No
Estate Tax...Yes
  Limited to federal estate tax collection.

PERSONAL INCOME TAXES

State Income Tax (%) ....3 - 7
  6 income brackets - Lowest $2,670; Highest $13,350.

Personal Exemption $ (single / joint) ....3,500 / 7,000
Standard Deduction $ (single / joint).........5,450 / 10,900
Federal Income Tax Paid - Deduction Allowed .... None
Social Security Income - Tax Exempt.................................Yes
Retired Military Pay - Tax Exempt .... Limits
State & Local Government Pensions - Tax Exempt .. Limits

Federal Civil Service Pensions - Tax Exempt .... Limits
Railroad Retirement - Tax Exempt ....Yes
Private Pension - Tax Exempt ....Limits

Note: Limits include a maximum combined exemption of $3,000 ($10,000 if 65 or older) from all retirement income sources.

VEHICLES

Registration Fees .... 2 Years
   Cars and RV's, $24.
   Utility or camper trailer, $10.
   Trucks, rate based on weight:
   0 - 6,000 lbs, $30 - $60.
   6,001 - 10,000 lbs, $70 - $100.

Annual Vehicle Tax ....Yes
   Annual property tax on vehicles.

State Emissions Test Required .... No
Vehicle Safety Inspection Required .... No
Mandatory Minimum Liability Insurance 25/50/25
   Uninsured Motorist coverage is also required.

COST OF LIVING INDICATORS

Rank: 1 highest; 51 lowest

Cost of Living - average statewide (rank) 27
Per Capita Income (rank / $) .... 46 / 31,884
Median Household Income (rank / $) .... 41 / 44,695
Median House Value (rank / $).......................... 36 / 131,000
Median Property Tax on Homes (rank) 46
Fuel - avg per gal $, Mar 2010 (diesel / gas).....2.74 / 2.56
Fuel Taxes - per gallon $ (diesel / gas)...........0.412 / 0.352
Cigarette Tax - pack of 20 ($) 1.08
Tax Burden - average all taxes (rank).................................. 38

STATE & LOCAL REVENUE SOURCES

Rank: 1 highest; 51 lowest
Rank and % of total revenue from:

Tax Revenue (see "Details" listed below) ....46 / 34.98
Charges & Misc. Revenue...03 / 26.49
Federal Government ....19 / 17.89
Utility Revenue...05 / 07.49
Insurance Trust Revenue...40 / 13.16

   Tax Revenue Details (rank / %)
Property Tax..18 / 31.11
Sales & Gross Receipts ....24 / 35.24

Individual Income Tax..27 / 23.47
Corporate Income Tax..43 / 02.26
Motor Vehicle License..34 / 01.35
Other Taxes ....21 / 06.57

POPULATION

Rank: 1 highest; 51 lowest

State Population (rank / count) .... 24 / 4,561,242
Population Per Square Mile (rank / count) .... 20 / 142

VOTING

Registration Requirements: In-person registration deadline is 30 days before election.

Address Requirements: Physical/street address required.

Register by Mail: Yes, registration deadline is 30 days before election.

Absentee Voting: Yes, excuse required.

Web Site: www.scvotes.org/

RESOURCES

South Carolina State Government
Phone: 866-340-7105
Web Site: www.myscgov.com

South Carolina Department of Revenue
Phone: 803-898-5709
Web Site: www.sctax.org

South Carolina Department of Motor Vehicles
Phone: 803-896-5000
Web Site: scdmvonline.com

South Carolina Office of Tourism
Phone: 888-727-6453
Web Site: www.discoversouthcarolina.com

South Dakota

WEATHER

	Rapid City			Sioux Falls		
	🌡	💧	❄	🌡	💧	❄
Jan	34/10	0.4	5	25/5	0.6	6.4
Feb	38/15	0.5	6.4	30/10	0.8	8.1
Mar	45/22	1	8.8	42/22	1.6	9.6
Apr	58/32	1.8	6.1	58/35	2.5	2.2
May	68/43	2.7	0.8	71/47	3.3	0
Jun	78/52	3	0.1	80/57	4	0
Jul	86/58	2	0	86/62	2.9	0
Aug	86/57	1.5	0	84/60	3.3	0
Sep	75/46	1.1	0.1	74/49	2.8	0
Oct	63/36	1	1.6	62/37	1.6	0.7
Nov	47/23	0.6	5.1	43/23	1	5.4
Dec	37/14	0.4	5.1	30/11	0.7	7.2

🌡	Average monthly high and low temperatures in degrees Fahrenheit.
💧	Average monthly precipitation totals in inches.
❄	Average monthly snowfall totals in inches.

STATE AND LOCAL TAXES

State Sales Tax (%) 4.00
Prescription drugs exempt. There is an 3% Excise Tax on vehicle purchases in lieu of sales tax, due with registration.

Local Sales Taxes (up to an additional %) 2.75
Inheritance Tax .... No
Estate Tax...Yes
Limited to federal estate tax collection.

PERSONAL INCOME TAXES

State Income Tax (%) .... None
Personal Exemption $ (single / joint) .... n/a
Standard Deduction $ (single / joint)..................... n/a
Federal Income Tax Paid - Deduction Allowed .... n/a
Social Security Income - Tax Exempt................................ n/a

Retired Military Pay - Tax Exempt .... n/a
State & Local Government Pensions - Tax Exempt .... n/a
Federal Civil Service Pensions - Tax Exempt .... n/a
Railroad Retirement - Tax Exempt .... n/a
Private Pension - Tax Exempt .... n/a

VEHICLES

Registration Fees .... 1 Year
Registration fees are based on weight and age of vehicle.

Cars, pickups, and vans. 0 to 4 years old:
1 - 10,000 lbs, $30 - $65.

Cars, pickups, and vans. 5 or more years old:
1 - 10,000 lbs, $21 - $45.50.

Travel trailer, 0 - 4 years old:
1 - 2,000 lbs, $10 - $20.
2,001 - 3,000 lbs, $35.
Each additional 1,000 lbs, $10

Travel trailer, 5 years old or more:
1 - 2,000 lbs, $7 - $14.
2,001 - 3,000 lbs, $24.50.
Each additional 1,000 lbs, $7.

Motor home, 0 - 4 years old:
1 - 6,000 lbs, $60.
Each additional 2,000 lbs, $20.

Motor home, 5 years old or more:
1 - 6,000 lbs, $42.
Each additional 2,000 lbs, $14.

Annual Vehicle Tax .... No
No property tax on vehicles.

State Emissions Test Required .... No
Vehicle Safety Inspection Required .... No
Mandatory Minimum Liability Insurance 25/50/25
Uninsured Motorist coverage is also required.

COST OF LIVING INDICATORS

Rank: 1 highest; 51 lowest

Cost of Living - average statewide (rank) 43
Per Capita Income (rank / $) .... 27 / 37,375
Median Household Income (rank / $) ....39 / 46,244
Median House Value (rank / $)........................43 / 118,400
Median Property Tax on Homes (rank) 28
Fuel - avg per gal $, Mar 2010 (diesel / gas) .....2.89 / 2.72

Fuel Taxes - per gallon $ (diesel / gas)............0.484 / 0.424
Cigarette Tax - pack of 20 ($) 2.54
Tax Burden - average all taxes (rank) 46

STATE & LOCAL REVENUE SOURCES

Rank: 1 highest; 51 lowest

Rank and % of total revenue from:

Tax Revenue (see "Details" listed below) ....47 / 33.84
Charges & Misc. Revenue...33 / 19.07
Federal Government ....11 / 20.00
Utility Revenue...25 / 03.28
Insurance Trust Revenue...05 / 23.82

Tax Revenue Details (rank / %)

Property Tax...14 / 34.30
Sales & Gross Receipts ....04 / 54.08
Individual Income Tax..44 / 0
Corporate Income Tax...34 / 03.21
Motor Vehicle License...12 / 02.46
Other Taxes ....24 / 05.95

POPULATION

Rank: 1 highest; 51 lowest

State Population (rank / count) ....46 / 812,383
Population Per Square Mile (rank / count) .... 47 / 11

VOTING

Registration Requirements: In-person registration deadline is 15 days before election.

Address Requirements: Physical/street address required.

Register by Mail: Yes, registration deadline is 15 days before election.

Absentee Voting: Yes, no excuse is required.

Web Site: www.sdsos.gov/electionsvoteregistration/electionsvoteregistration_overview.shtm

RESOURCES

South Dakota State Government
Phone: 605-773-3011
Web Site: www.state.sd.us

South Dakota Department of Revenue and Regulation
Phone: 605-773-3311
Web Site: www.state.sd.us/revenue

South Dakota Driver Licensing Program
Phone: 605-773-6883
Web Site: www.state.sd.us/dps/dl

South Dakota Motor Vehicles Division
Phone: 605-773-3541
Web Site: www.state.sd.us/drr2/motorvehicle

South Dakota Office of Tourism
Phone: 800-732-5682
Web Site: www.travelsd.com

Tennessee

WEATHER

	Memphis			Nashville		
	🌡	💧	❄	🌡	💧	❄
Jan	49/32	4.7	2.3	47/28	4.3	3.8
Feb	54/35	4.5	1.3	51/31	4.2	3.1
Mar	62/43	5.2	0.8	60/39	5	1.4
Apr	73/52	5.6	0	71/48	4	0
May	81/61	4.9	0	79/57	4.6	0
Jun	89/69	3.9	0	87/65	3.8	0
Jul	92/73	3.9	0	90/69	3.8	0
Aug	90/71	3.4	0	89/68	3.3	0
Sep	84/64	3.2	0	83/61	3.4	0
Oct	74/52	2.9	0	72/48	2.7	0
Nov	62/42	4.8	0.1	60/39	3.9	0.4
Dec	52/35	5.3	0.6	50/31	4.6	1.5
🌡	Average monthly high and low temperatures in degrees Fahrenheit.					
💧	Average monthly precipitation totals in inches.					
❄	Average monthly snowfall totals in inches.					

STATE AND LOCAL TAXES

State Sales Tax (%) 7.00
Prescription drugs exempt. Food is taxed at 5.5%.

Local Sales Taxes (up to an additional %) 2.75

Inheritance Tax ....Yes
Ranges from 5.5% to 9.5%. Spouses are exempt.

Estate Tax ....Yes
Limited to federal estate tax collection.

PERSONAL INCOME TAXES

State Income Tax (%) .... None
State income tax applies only to dividend and interest income. The first $1,250 ($2,500 for joint filers) is exempt. Persons 65 and older may exclude $16,200 single, $27,000 married filing jointly.

Personal Exemption $ (single / joint) .... n/a
Standard Deduction $ (single / joint) .... n/a

Federal Income Tax Paid - Deduction Allowed .... n/a
Social Security Income - Tax Exempt .... n/a
Retired Military Pay - Tax Exempt .... n/a
State & Local Government Pensions - Tax Exempt .... n/a
Federal Civil Service Pensions - Tax Exempt .... n/a
Railroad Retirement - Tax Exempt .... n/a
Private Pension - Tax Exempt .... n/a

VEHICLES

Registration Fees .... 1 Year
Vehicle registrations are processed at a local county clerk's office. Basic fee around $10 - $30. Based on type of vehicle.

A "Privilege Tax" is also charged in some counties. Fees are around $20 - $80.

Annual Vehicle Tax .... No
No property tax on vehicles.

State Emissions Test Required ....Yes
Annual for all gas or diesel-fueled vehicles up to 10,500 lbs in Davidson, Hamilton, Rutherford, Sumner, Williamson, and Wilson counties.
Web Site: www.state.tn.us/environment/apc/vehicle.

Vehicle Safety Inspection Required .... No
Mandatory Minimum Liability Insurance 25/50/15

COST OF LIVING INDICATORS

Rank: 1 highest; 51 lowest

Cost of Living - average statewide (rank) 50
Per Capita Income (rank / $) ....38 / 34,330
Median Household Income (rank / $) ....45 / 43,610
Median House Value (rank / $)........................37 / 130,900
Median Property Tax on Homes (rank) 42
Fuel - avg per gal $, Mar 2010 (diesel / gas).....2.77 / 2.60
Fuel Taxes - per gallon $ (diesel / gas)...........0.428 / 0.398
Cigarette Tax - pack of 20 ($) 1.63
Tax Burden - average all taxes (rank) 45

STATE & LOCAL REVENUE SOURCES

Rank: 1 highest; 51 lowest
Rank and % of total revenue from:

Tax Revenue (see "Details" listed below) ....45 / 35.21
Charges & Misc. Revenue...18 / 21.43
Federal Government ....21 / 17.10
Utility Revenue ....02 / 14.81
Insurance Trust Revenue...46 / 11.45

Tax Revenue Details (rank / %)

Property Tax...38 / 23.83
Sales & Gross Receipts ....03 / 57.07
Individual Income Tax................................43 / 01.38
Corporate Income Tax...............................11 / 06.10
Motor Vehicle License................................09 / 02.54
Other Taxes ....15 / 09.08

POPULATION

Rank: 1 highest; 51 lowest

State Population (rank / count) ....17 / 6,296,254
Population Per Square Mile (rank / count) ....18 / 149

VOTING

Registration Requirements: In-person registration deadline is 30 days before election.

Address Requirements: Physical/street address required.

Register by Mail: Yes, registration deadline is 30 days before election.

Absentee Voting: Yes, excuse required.

Web Site: www.state.tn.us/sos/election/

RESOURCES

Tennessee State Government
Phone: 615-313-0300
Web Site: www.tn.gov

Tennessee Department of Revenue
Phone: 615-253-0600
Web Site: www.tn.gov/revenue

Tennessee Department of Safety (Driver License)
Phone: 615-253-5221
Web Site: www.tn.gov/safety/dlmain.htm

Tennessee Vehicle Services
Phone: 615-741-3101
Web Site: www.state.tn.us/revenue/vehicle

Tennessee Office of Tourism
Phone: 800-462-8366
Web Site: www.tnvacation.com

Texas

WEATHER

	Dallas			Houston		
	🌡	💧	❄	🌡	💧	❄
Jan	54/34	1.9	1.2	61/41	3.9	0.2
Feb	60/38	2.2	1	66/44	2.9	0.2
Mar	68/45	2.6	0.2	73/51	3.5	0
Apr	76/55	3.8	0	79/58	3.6	0
May	83/63	5	0	85/65	5.6	0
Jun	92/71	2.9	0	91/71	5.1	0
Jul	96/75	2.2	0	94/73	3.4	0
Aug	96/74	2	0	93/73	3.7	0
Sep	88/67	3	0	89/68	4.3	0
Oct	79/56	3.5	0	82/59	4.7	0
Nov	66/45	2.2	0.1	72/50	3.7	0
Dec	58/37	1.9	0.2	65/44	3.6	0
🌡	Average monthly high and low temperatures in degrees Fahrenheit.					
💧	Average monthly precipitation totals in inches.					
❄	Average monthly snowfall totals in inches.					

STATE AND LOCAL TAXES

State Sales Tax (%)...6.25
Exempt: food and prescription drugs. Texas also has a 1% (0.5% for retailers) franchise tax in addition to the sales tax.

Local Sales Taxes (up to an additional %) 2.00
Inheritance Tax ....No
Estate Tax..Yes
Limited to federal estate tax collection.

PERSONAL INCOME TAXES

State Income Tax (%) ....None
Personal Exemption $ (single / joint) ....n/a
Standard Deduction $ (single / joint)..............................n/a
Federal Income Tax Paid - Deduction Allowed ....n/a
Social Security Income - Tax Exempt................................n/a
Retired Military Pay - Tax Exempt ....n/a

State & Local Government Pensions - Tax Exempt .... n/a
Federal Civil Service Pensions - Tax Exempt .... n/a
Railroad Retirement - Tax Exempt .... n/a
Private Pension - Tax Exempt .... n/a

VEHICLES

Registration Fees .... 1 Year
All passenger vehicles under 6,000 lbs, $40.80 - $58. Rate varies by year.

For vehicles 6,001 lbs and over. Base fee of $25 plus 60 cents per hundred pounds.

Light trucks, carrying capacity of one ton or less. Fee based on gross weight of vehicle:
901 - 4,000 lbs, $29.70 - $42.90.
4,001 - 8,000 lbs, $43.34 - $64.90.

There is a Local Fee of $5 to $20 in addition to registration fee. The fee varies by county.

A new Texas resident must pay a $90 use tax on a motor vehicle previously registered in another state.

Annual Vehicle Tax .... No
No property tax on vehicles.

State Emissions Test Required ....Yes
Annual for vehicles in Brazoria, Fort Bend, Galveston, Harris, Montgomery, Collin, Dallas, Denton, Ellis, Johnson, Kaufman, Parker, Rockwell, Tarrant, Travis, Williamson and El Paso counties. Diesel powered vehicles are exempt. Web Site: www.txdps.state.tx.us/vi.

Vehicle Safety Inspection Required ....Yes
Annual.

Mandatory Minimum Liability Insurance 25/50/25
Minimum coverage requirements will increase to 30/60/25 on January 1, 2011.

COST OF LIVING INDICATORS

Rank: 1 highest; 51 lowest

Cost of Living - average statewide (rank) 47
Per Capita Income (rank / $) .... 24 / 38,575
Median Household Income (rank / $) .... 28 / 50,049
Median House Value (rank / $)........................ 41 / 120,500
Median Property Tax on Homes (rank) 14
Fuel - avg per gal $, Mar 2010 (diesel / gas) .....2.76 / 2.57
Fuel Taxes - per gallon $ (diesel / gas)...........0.444 / 0.384
Cigarette Tax - pack of 20 ($) 2.42
Tax Burden - average all taxes (rank) 44

STATE & LOCAL REVENUE SOURCES

Rank: 1 highest; 51 lowest
Rank and % of total revenue from:

Tax Revenue (see "Details" listed below) ....23 / 41.86
Charges & Misc. Revenue.......................................16 / 21.88
Federal Government ....29 / 15.84
Utility Revenue..11 / 05.42
Insurance Trust Revenue..33 / 15.00

Tax Revenue Details (rank / %)

Property Tax...04 / 41.68
Sales & Gross Receipts ....13 / 46.73
Individual Income Tax...44 / 0
Corporate Income Tax...46 / 0
Motor Vehicle License...16 / 02.13
Other Taxes ....12 / 09.46

POPULATION

Rank: 1 highest; 51 lowest

State Population (rank / count) ....02 / 24,782,302
Population Per Square Mile (rank / count) .... 25 / 92

VOTING

Registration Requirements: In-person registration deadline is 30 days before election.

Address Requirements: Physical/street address required.

Register by Mail: Yes, registration deadline is 30 days before election.

Absentee Voting: Yes, excuse required.

Web Site: www.sos.state.tx.us/elections/index.shtml

RESOURCES

Texas State Government
Phone: 512-463-5455
Web Site: www.texasonline.com

Texas Comptroller of Public Accounts
Phone: 877-662-8375
Web Site: www.window.state.tx.us

Texas Department of Public Safety (Driver License)
Phone: 512-424-2000
Web Site: www.txdps.state.tx.us

Texas Department of Transportation (Title &
Registration)
Phone: 800-558-9368
Web Site: www.dot.state.tx.us

Texas Office of Tourism
Phone: 800-888-8839
Web Site: www.traveltex.com

Utah

WEATHER

	Saint George			Salt Lake City		
	🌡	💧	❄	🌡	💧	❄
Jan	53/24	1	N/A	37/20	1.3	13.5
Feb	59/29	1	N/A	43/24	1.2	9.4
Mar	67/35	0.9	N/A	52/31	1.8	9.4
Apr	76/42	0.5	N/A	62/38	2	5
May	85/49	0.4	N/A	72/46	1.8	0.6
Jun	96/57	0.2	N/A	83/54	0.9	0
Jul	101/65	0.8	N/A	92/62	0.7	0
Aug	99/63	0.8	N/A	90/61	0.8	0
Sep	93/53	0.6	N/A	80/51	1.1	0.1
Oct	80/41	0.7	N/A	66/40	1.3	1.3
Nov	65/30	0.5	N/A	50/30	1.3	6.6
Dec	54/24	0.8	N/A	39/22	1.3	12

🌡	Average monthly high and low temperatures in degrees Fahrenheit.
💧	Average monthly precipitation totals in inches.
❄	Average monthly snowfall totals in inches.

STATE AND LOCAL TAXES

State Sales Tax (%) 5.95
   Includes 1.25% in local & county sales tax that is collected
      statewide. Exempt: prescription drugs.

Local Sales Taxes (up to an additional %) 2.40
Inheritance Tax .... No
Estate Tax ....Yes
   Limited to federal estate tax collection.

PERSONAL INCOME TAXES

State Income Tax (%) 5
   Flat tax, no income brackets.

Personal Exemption $ (single / joint) ....2,738 / 5,516
Standard Deduction $ (single / joint) ....See note
   Deduction is a tax credit of 6% of federal amount and
   phases out at 1.3 cents per dollar above $12,510 adjusted
   gross income, $25,022 for joint return.

Federal Income Tax Paid - Deduction Allowed .... None
Social Security Income - Tax Exempt .... Limits
Retired Military Pay - Tax Exempt .... Limits
State & Local Government Pensions - Tax Exempt .. Limits
Federal Civil Service Pensions - Tax Exempt .... Limits
Railroad Retirement - Tax Exempt .... Limits
Private Pension - Tax Exempt .... Limits

Note: A tax credit up to $450 may be available, amount phases-out with higher income levels. Age and date restrictions also apply.

VEHICLES

Registration Fees .... 1 Year
Vehicle registration fee varies depending on vehicle type, fuel type, county, and other factors. To find out the amount for your vehicle call the DMV at 801-297-7780 or 1-800-368-8824.

Annual Vehicle Tax ....Yes
The vehicle property assessment fee is a uniform fee based on the age of the vehicle. These fees are paid at time of vehicle registration. Below are rates for the most common types of vehicles.

Passenger Vehicles:
Less than 3 years old, $150.
3 - 5 years old, $110.
6 - 9 years old, $80.
9 - 11 years old, $50.
12 or more years old, $10.

Travel Trailers:
Less than 3 years old, $175.
3 - 5 years old, $135.
6 - 9 years old, $90.
9 - 11 years old, $65.
12 or more years old, $20.

Tent Trailers and Truck Campers:
Less than 3 years old, $70.
3 - 5 years old, $50.
6 - 9 years old, $35.
9 - 11 years old, $25.
12 or more years old, $10.

Motor homes are subject to a uniform fee of 1% of the fair market value as established by the Tax Commission.

State Emissions Test Required ....Yes
Every two years for vehicles less than six years old,
annual for vehicles over six years old. In Davis, Salt Lake, Utah, and Weber counties only. Web Site: http://dmv. utah.gov/registerinspections.html#emission.

Vehicle Safety Inspection Required ....Yes
Every two years for vehicles less than eight years old, annual for vehicles eight or more years old.

Mandatory Minimum Liability Insurance 25/65/15
Personal Injury Protection is also required.

COST OF LIVING INDICATORS
Rank: 1 highest; 51 lowest

Cost of Living - average statewide (rank) 29
Per Capita Income (rank / $) ....50 / 30,291
Median Household Income (rank / $) .... 15 / 56,820
Median House Value (rank / $) ....20 / 215,200
Median Property Tax on Homes (rank) 33
Fuel - avg per gal $, Mar 2010 (diesel / gas) .....2.90 / 2.74
Fuel Taxes - per gallon $ (diesel / gas) ....0.489 / 0.429
Cigarette Tax - pack of 20 ($) 1.71
Tax Burden - average all taxes (rank) 23

STATE & LOCAL REVENUE SOURCES
Rank: 1 highest; 51 lowest
Rank and % of total revenue from:

Tax Revenue (see "Details" listed below) ....37 / 38.40
Charges & Misc. Revenue..05 / 25.53
Federal Government ....36 / 14.91
Utility Revenue ....06 / 07.33
Insurance Trust Revenue..36 / 13.83

Tax Revenue Details (rank / %)

Property Tax..40 / 22.89
Sales & Gross Receipts ....14 / 39.12
Individual Income Tax..14 / 28.75
Corporate Income Tax..22 / 04.48
Motor Vehicle License...35 / 01.19
Other Taxes ....41 / 03.57

POPULATION
Rank: 1 highest; 51 lowest

State Population (rank / count) ....34 / 2,784,572
Population Per Square Mile (rank / count) .... 42 / 33

VOTING

Registration Requirements: In-person registration deadline is 15 days before election.

Address Requirements: Physical/street address required.

Register by Mail: Yes, registration deadline is 30 days before election.

Absentee Voting: Yes, no excuse is required.

Web Site: http://elections.utah.gov/

RESOURCES

Utah State Government
Phone: 801-538-3000
Web Site: www.utah.gov

Utah State Tax Commission
Phone: 801-297-2200
Web Site: www.tax.utah.gov

Utah Driver License Division
Phone: 801-965-4461
Web Site: www.publicsafety.utah.gov/dld

Utah Division of Motor Vehicles
Phone: 801-297-3570
Web Site: www.dmv.utah.gov

Utah Office of Tourism
Phone: 800-200-1160
Web Site: www.utah.com

Vermont

WEATHER

	Burlington		
	🌡	💧	❄
Jan	26/8	1.8	18.8
Feb	28/10	1.7	16.8
Mar	38/21	2.2	12.4
Apr	53/33	2.8	3.8
May	67/44	3	0.2
Jun	76/54	3.3	0
Jul	81/59	3.6	0
Aug	78/57	4	0
Sep	69/49	3.3	0
Oct	57/39	3	0.2
Nov	44/30	3	6.6
Dec	31/16	2.3	18.1
🌡	Average monthly high and low temperatures in degrees Fahrenheit.		
💧	Average monthly precipitation totals in inches.		
❄	Average monthly snowfall totals in inches.		

STATE AND LOCAL TAXES

State Sales Tax (%) 6.00
   Exempt: food and prescription drugs.

Local Sales Taxes (up to an additional %) 1.00
Inheritance Tax .... No
Estate Tax...Yes
   Some exceptions.

PERSONAL INCOME TAXES

State Income Tax (%) ....3.55 - 8.95
   5 income brackets - Lowest $33,950; Highest $372,950.

Personal Exemption $ (single / joint) ....3,500 / 7,000
Standard Deduction $ (single / joint)......... 5,450 / 10,900
Federal Income Tax Paid - Deduction Allowed .... None
Social Security Income - Tax Exempt............................Limits
   Taxable to extent federally taxed.

Retired Military Pay - Tax Exempt .... No

State & Local Government Pensions - Tax Exempt .... No
Federal Civil Service Pensions - Tax Exempt .... No
Railroad Retirement - Tax Exempt ....Yes
Private Pension - Tax Exempt .... No

VEHICLES

Registration Fees .... 1 Year
 Cars, Trucks (up to 6,099 lbs), and Motor homes:
 Gas powered, $65.
 Diesel powered, $27.

 If sales tax was not paid to another state on the purchase of the vehicle Vermont will charge a 6% sales tax. If amount paid was less than 6% you will be charged the difference. You may claim a tax credit for a vehicle registered to you for a period of 3 years or more where you paid a state sales or use tax on the vehicle.

Annual Vehicle Tax .... No
 No property tax on vehicles.

State Emissions Test Required ....Yes
 Annual with safety inspection. Vehicles over 8,500 lbs GVWR are exempt. Web Site: http://dmv.vermont.gov/safety/detailedinformation.

Vehicle Safety Inspection Required ....Yes
 Annual.

Mandatory Minimum Liability Insurance 25/50/10

COST OF LIVING INDICATORS

 Rank: 1 highest; 51 lowest

Cost of Living - average statewide (rank) 10
Per Capita Income (rank / $) .... 23 / 38,880
Median Household Income (rank / $) .... 21 / 52,111
Median House Value (rank / $)........................ 23 / 203,800
Median Property Tax on Homes (rank) 08
Fuel - avg per gal $, Mar 2010 (diesel / gas).....3.05 / 2.75
Fuel Taxes - per gallon $ (diesel / gas)...........0.534 / 0.429
Cigarette Tax - pack of 20 ($) 3.25
Tax Burden - average all taxes (rank).................................. 09

STATE & LOCAL REVENUE SOURCES

 Rank: 1 highest; 51 lowest
 Rank and % of total revenue from:

Tax Revenue (see "Details" listed below) ....07 / 46.06
Charges & Misc. Revenue..36 / 18.10
Federal Government ....05 / 22.56
Utility Revenue..26 / 03.26
Insurance Trust Revenue...49 / 10.02

Tax Revenue Details (rank / %)

Property Tax...02 / 42.19
Sales & Gross Receipts ....36 / 29.21
Individual Income Tax...34 / 19.83
Corporate Income Tax...39 / 02.84
Motor Vehicle License...08 / 02.59
Other Taxes..44 / 03.34

POPULATION

 Rank: 1 highest; 51 lowest

State Population (rank / count) ....49 / 621,760
Population Per Square Mile (rank / count) .... 31 / 65

VOTING

Registration Requirements: In-person registration deadline is 7 days before election.

Address Requirements: Physical/street address required.

Register by Mail: Yes, registration deadline is 7 days before election.

Absentee Voting: Yes, no excuse is required.

Web Site: www.vermont-elections.org/

RESOURCES

Vermont State Government
Phone: 802-828-1110
Web Site: www.vermont.gov

Vermont Department of Taxes
Phone: 802-828-2505
Web Site: www.state.vt.us/tax

Vermont Department of Motor Vehicles
Phone: 802-828-2000
Web Site: www.dmv.state.vt.us

Vermont Office of Tourism
Phone: 800-837-6668
Web Site: www.vermontvacation.com

Virginia

WEATHER

	Norfolk			Richmond		
	🌡	💧	❄	🌡	💧	❄
Jan	48/32	3.6	2.6	47/28	3.3	4.9
Feb	51/33	3.3	2.9	50/30	2.9	4.1
Mar	58/40	3.8	1	59/37	3.7	2.4
Apr	68/48	3	0	69/45	3.1	0.1
May	76/57	3.7	0	78/55	3.7	0
Jun	84/66	3.5	0	85/63	3.6	0
Jul	88/71	5.2	0	88/68	5.1	0
Aug	86/70	5.3	0	87/67	4.8	0
Sep	80/64	3.9	0	81/60	3.3	0
Oct	70/53	3.3	0	71/48	3.1	0
Nov	61/44	3	0	60/39	2.9	0.4
Dec	52/35	3.1	0.9	50/31	3.1	2

🌡	Average monthly high and low temperatures in degrees Fahrenheit.
💧	Average monthly precipitation totals in inches.
❄	Average monthly snowfall totals in inches.

STATE AND LOCAL TAXES

State Sales Tax (%) 5.00
Includes a 1% local tax collected statewide. Exempt: prescription drugs.

Local Sales Taxes (up to an additional %) .... None
Inheritance Tax .... No
Estate Tax .... No

PERSONAL INCOME TAXES

State Income Tax (%) ....2 - 5.75
4 income brackets - Lowest $3,000; Highest $17,000.

Personal Exemption $ (single / joint) .... 930 / 1,860
Standard Deduction $ (single / joint) ....3,000 / 6,000
Federal Income Tax Paid - Deduction Allowed .... None
Social Security Income - Tax Exempt ....Yes
Retired Military Pay - Tax Exempt .... Limits
State & Local Government Pensions - Tax Exempt .. Limits
Federal Civil Service Pensions - Tax Exempt .... Limits

Railroad Retirement - Tax Exempt ....Yes
Private Pension - Tax Exempt .... Limits

Note: Limits include a maximum combined exemption of $12,000 (if 65 or older) from all retirement income sources. Some income limitations.

VEHICLES

Registration Fees .... 1 Year
Passenger cars and motor homes $38.75 - $43.75, depending on weight.

Pickup truck $38.75 - $49.75, depending on weight.

Travel trailer, $29.50.

The city of Virginia Beach is the only location that currently participates in the "Local Vehicle Registration Program". This city adds an additional $25 to $30 to the standard registration fee.

Annual Vehicle Tax ....Yes
Annual property tax on vehicles.

State Emissions Test Required ....Yes
Every two years. Operated primarily in the counties of Arlington, Fairfax, Loudoun, Prince William, and Stafford, or the cities of Alexandria, Fairfax, Falls Church, Manassas, and Manassas Park. Web Site: www.dmv. virginia.gov/webdoc/citizen/vehicles/emissions.asp.

Vehicle Safety Inspection Required ....Yes
Annual.

Mandatory Minimum Liability Insurance 25/50/20
Uninsured and Underinsured Motorists coverage is also required.

COST OF LIVING INDICATORS

Rank: 1 highest; 51 lowest

Cost of Living - average statewide (rank) 26
Per Capita Income (rank / $) .... 09 / 42,876
Median Household Income (rank / $) .... 08 / 61,210
Median House Value (rank / $) ....13 / 259,200
Median Property Tax on Homes (rank) 23
Fuel - avg per gal $, Mar 2010 (diesel / gas) .....2.81 / 2.61
Fuel Taxes - per gallon $ (diesel / gas) ....0.425 / 0.365
Plus 2.1% sales tax in some areas.

Cigarette Tax - pack of 20 ($) 1.31
Tax Burden - average all taxes (rank) 19

STATE & LOCAL REVENUE SOURCES

Rank: 1 highest; 51 lowest

Rank and % of total revenue from:

Tax Revenue (see "Details" listed below) ....08 / 45.92
Charges & Misc. Revenue.................................15 / 22.12
Federal Government ....51 / 10.61
Utility Revenue..33 / 02.44
Insurance Trust Revenue.................................17 / 18.91

Tax Revenue Details (rank / %)

Property Tax..20 / 30.94
Sales & Gross Receipts ....40 / 26.37
Individual Income Tax.....................................06 / 31.63
Corporate Income Tax.....................................40 / 02.72
Motor Vehicle License......................................25 / 01.59
Other Taxes...20 / 06.75

POPULATION

Rank: 1 highest; 51 lowest

State Population (rank / count) ....12 / 7,882,590
Population Per Square Mile (rank / count) ....14 / 184

VOTING

Registration Requirements: In-person registration deadline is 29 days before election.

Address Requirements: Physical/street address required.

Register by Mail: Yes, registration deadline is 29 days before election.

Absentee Voting: Yes, excuse required.

Web Site: www.sbe.virginia.gov/cms/

RESOURCES

Virginia State Government
Phone: 877-482-3468
Web Site: www.virginia.gov

Virginia Department of Taxation
Phone: 804-367-8031
Web Site: www.tax.virginia.gov

Virginia Department of Motor Vehicles
Phone: 866-368-5463
Web Site: www.dmv.virginia.gov

Virginia Office of Tourism
Phone: 800-847-4882
Web Site: www.virginia.org

Washington

WEATHER

	Seattle			Vancouver		
	🌡	💧	❄	🌡	💧	❄
Jan	45/36	5.1	3	44/32	5.7	4.2
Feb	49/38	3.7	0.9	49/34	4.5	1.5
Mar	53/40	3.3	0.6	55/37	3.8	0.3
Apr	58/43	2.2	0	61/40	2.7	0
May	64/48	1.7	0	67/45	2.2	0
Jun	69/53	1.4	0	72/50	1.7	0
Jul	74/56	0.7	0	78/53	0.6	0
Aug	74/56	0.9	0	79/53	0.9	0
Sep	68/53	1.6	0	73/49	1.9	0
Oct	60/48	3	0	63/43	3.2	0
Nov	51/42	5.1	0.7	52/38	6	0.1
Dec	47/38	5.4	1.9	45/34	6.3	1
🌡	Average monthly high and low temperatures in degrees Fahrenheit.					
💧	Average monthly precipitation totals in inches.					
❄	Average monthly snowfall totals in inches.					

STATE AND LOCAL TAXES

State Sales Tax (%)..6.50
Washington also has a gross receipts tax called the Business and Occupation Tax which is levied at various rates. Retail sales are 0.471%. Exempt: food and prescription drugs.

Local Sales Taxes (up to an additional %) 2.40
Inheritance Tax .... No
Estate Tax..Yes
On estates valued at $2 million or more.

PERSONAL INCOME TAXES

State Income Tax (%).. None
Personal Exemption $ (single / joint) .... n/a
Standard Deduction $ (single / joint)............................... n/a
Federal Income Tax Paid - Deduction Allowed .... n/a
Social Security Income - Tax Exempt.............................. n/a
Retired Military Pay - Tax Exempt .... n/a

State & Local Government Pensions - Tax Exempt .... n/a
Federal Civil Service Pensions - Tax Exempt .... n/a
Railroad Retirement - Tax Exempt .... n/a
Private Pension - Tax Exempt .... n/a

VEHICLES

Registration Fees .... 1 Year
Vehicle fees are based on several factors including the vehicle weight and where you live.

Vehicles from 0 to 8,000 lbs, $43.75 - $63.75.

Motor home, $75.

Travel trailer, $30.

Trucks:
0 - 8,000 lbs, $41 - $61.
8,001 - 12,000 lbs, $63 - $80.

If you live in the areas of King, Pierce, or Snohomish counties you may be required to pay the Regional Transit Authority (RTA) tax. The RTA is an annual excise tax of 0.3% based on the value of your vehicle.

City or county governments can also impose an annual "Local Transportation Benefit District Fee", due with the registration. There are currently 5 areas charging this fee which adds an additional $20 per vehicle.

Annual Vehicle Tax .... No
No property tax on vehicles.

State Emissions Test Required ....Yes
Every two years in Clark, King, Pierce, Snohomish, and Spokane counties.
Web Site: www.emissiontestwa.com/index.aspx.

Vehicle Safety Inspection Required .... No
Mandatory Minimum Liability Insurance 25/50/10

COST OF LIVING INDICATORS

Rank: 1 highest; 51 lowest

Cost of Living - average statewide (rank) 18
Per Capita Income (rank / $) .... 15 / 42,356
Median Household Income (rank / $) .... 12 / 58,081
Median House Value (rank / $) .... 10 / 293,000
Median Property Tax on Homes (rank) 12
Fuel - avg per gal $, Mar 2010 (diesel / gas) .....3.06 / 2.91
Fuel Taxes - per gallon $ (diesel / gas) ....0.619 / 0.559
Cigarette Tax - pack of 20 ($) 3.04
Tax Burden - average all taxes (rank) 36

STATE & LOCAL REVENUE SOURCES

Rank: 1 highest; 51 lowest
Rank and % of total revenue from:

Tax Revenue (see "Details" listed below) ....38 / 38.07
Charges & Misc. Revenue...28 / 19.70
Federal Government ....47 / 12.32
Utility Revenue ....03 / 08.02
Insurance Trust Revenue...06 / 21.89

Tax Revenue Details (rank / %)

Property Tax..32 / 26.78
Sales & Gross Receipts ....01 / 62.05
Individual Income Tax...44 / 0
Corporate Income Tax...46 / 0
Motor Vehicle License...21 / 01.78
Other Taxes ....13 / 09.39

POPULATION

Rank: 1 highest; 51 lowest

State Population (rank / count) .... 13 / 6,664,195
Population Per Square Mile (rank / count) .... 24 / 93

VOTING

Registration Requirements: In-person registration deadline is 15 days before election.

Address Requirements: Physical/street address required.

Register by Mail: Yes, registration deadline is 30 days before election.

Absentee Voting: Yes, no excuse is required.

Web Site: www.secstate.wa.gov/elections/

RESOURCES

Washington State Government
Phone: 877-265-6553
Web Site: www.access.wa.gov

Washington State Department of Revenue
Phone: 800-647-7706
Web Site: www.dor.wa.gov

Washington State Department of Licensing
Phone: 360-902-3770
Web Site: www.dol.wa.gov

Washington Office of Tourism
Phone: 800-544-1800
Web Site: www.experiencewa.com

West Virginia

WEATHER

	Charleston			Morgantown		
	🌡	💧	❄	🌡	💧	❄
Jan	43/25	3.4	10.1	42/25	3.9	7.9
Feb	46/27	3.2	8.7	43/26	2.8	6.1
Mar	56/34	3.9	5.1	50/31	3	5.2
Apr	67/43	3.3	0.9	64/42	3.3	0.3
May	76/52	3.9	0	73/50	4	0
Jun	83/60	3.6	0	81/59	4.1	0
Jul	86/65	4.9	0	84/63	4.2	0
Aug	85/63	4	0	83/61	4.3	0
Sep	78/56	3.2	0	77/54	2.7	0
Oct	68/45	2.6	0.2	67/45	2.5	0
Nov	56/36	3.3	2.2	53/34	2.6	2.6
Dec	46/28	3.3	5.1	42/26	2.9	6

🌡	Average monthly high and low temperatures in degrees Fahrenheit.
💧	Average monthly precipitation totals in inches.
❄	Average monthly snowfall totals in inches.

STATE AND LOCAL TAXES

State Sales Tax (%) 6.00
Exempt: prescription drugs. Food is taxed at 3%.

Local Sales Taxes (up to an additional %) .... None
Inheritance Tax .... No
Estate Tax..Yes
Limited to federal estate tax collection.

PERSONAL INCOME TAXES

State Income Tax (%) .... 3 - 6.5
5 income brackets - Lowest $10,000; Highest $60,000.

Personal Exemption $ (single / joint) ....2,000 / 4,000
Standard Deduction $ (single / joint)............................ None
Federal Income Tax Paid - Deduction Allowed .... None
Social Security Income - Tax Exempt............................ Limits
Taxable to extent federally taxable.

Retired Military Pay - Tax Exempt ....Limits
First $2,000 is exempt. Balance based on formula with years of military service, maximum $22,000.

State & Local Government Pensions - Tax Exempt .. Limits
Up to $2,000 exempt.

Federal Civil Service Pensions - Tax Exempt .... Limits
Up to $2,000 is exempt. Full exemption for some law enforcement occupations.

Railroad Retirement - Tax Exempt ....Yes
Private Pension - Tax Exempt .... Limits
See note below.

Note: Taxpayers 65 and older may exclude the first $8,000 of any retirement income. Pension exemptions count toward the $8,000.

VEHICLES

Registration Fees .... 1 Year
Basic registration fee for passenger vehicles and pickup trucks weighing 8,000 lbs or less, $30.

Annual Vehicle Tax ....Yes
Annual property tax on vehicles.

State Emissions Test Required .... No
Vehicle Safety Inspection Required ....Yes
Annual.

Mandatory Minimum Liability Insurance 20/40/10
Uninsured Motorist coverage is also required.

COST OF LIVING INDICATORS

Rank: 1 highest; 51 lowest

Cost of Living - average statewide (rank) 35
Per Capita Income (rank / $) .... 49 / 30,831
Median Household Income (rank / $) .... 51 / 37,528
Median House Value (rank / $)........................... 51 / 93,500
Median Property Tax on Homes (rank) 49
Fuel - avg per gal $, Mar 2010 (diesel / gas).....2.94 / 2.74
Fuel Taxes - per gallon $ (diesel / gas)...........0.565 / 0.505
Cigarette Tax - pack of 20 ($) 1.56
Tax Burden - average all taxes (rank) 30

STATE & LOCAL REVENUE SOURCES

Rank: 1 highest; 51 lowest
Rank and % of total revenue from:

Tax Revenue (see "Details" listed below) ....25 / 41.19
Charges & Misc. Revenue...................................04 / 25.85

Federal Government ....04 / 23.07
Utility Revenue ....44 / 01.38
Insurance Trust Revenue.......................................50 / 08.52

Tax Revenue Details (rank / %)

Property Tax..44 / 18.62
Sales & Gross Receipts ....17 / 37.89
Individual Income Tax..33 / 22.29
Corporate Income Tax...04 / 08.83
Motor Vehicle License ....29 / 01.45
Other Taxes ....10 / 10.92

POPULATION

Rank: 1 highest; 51 lowest

State Population (rank / count) ....37 / 1,819,777
Population Per Square Mile (rank / count) ....30 / 75

VOTING

Registration Requirements: In-person registration deadline is 21 days before election.

Address Requirements: Physical/street address required.

Register by Mail: Yes, registration deadline is 21 days before election.

Absentee Voting: Yes, excuse required.

Web Site: www.wvsos.com/elections/main.htm

RESOURCES

West Virginia State Government
Phone: 304-558-3456
Web Site: www.wv.gov

West Virginia Department of Tax and Revenue
Phone: 304-558-0211
Web Site: www.wvrevenue.gov

West Virginia Division of Motor Vehicles
Phone: 304-558-3900
Web Site: www.transportation.wv.gov

West Virginia Office of Tourism
Phone: 800-225-5982
Web Site: www.callwva.com

Wisconsin

WEATHER

	Green Bay			Milwaukee		
	🌡	💧	❄	🌡	💧	❄
Jan	23/7	1.1	10.5	27/13	1.7	12.8
Feb	27/10	1	8.2	31/17	1.4	9.6
Mar	38/21	1.9	8.9	40/26	2.6	8.7
Apr	54/34	2.7	2.4	54/36	3.4	1.7
May	67/44	2.9	0.2	65/45	2.8	0.1
Jun	76/53	3.2	0	76/56	3.4	0
Jul	81/58	3.4	0	80/62	3.6	0
Aug	79/57	3.3	0	79/61	3.5	0
Sep	70/48	3.2	0	71/53	2.9	0
Oct	58/38	2.2	0.2	60/42	2.4	0.2
Nov	42/26	2.1	4.7	45/30	2.4	3
Dec	28/13	1.4	11	32/19	2.1	10.4
🌡	Average monthly high and low temperatures in degrees Fahrenheit.					
💧	Average monthly precipitation totals in inches.					
❄	Average monthly snowfall totals in inches.					

STATE AND LOCAL TAXES

State Sales Tax (%) 5.00
  Exempt: food and prescription drugs.

Local Sales Taxes (up to an additional %) 0.60
Inheritance Tax .... No
Estate Tax...See note.
  No estate tax through December 31, 2010. In 2011 estates of $1 million or more are required to file.

PERSONAL INCOME TAXES

State Income Tax (%) .... 4.6 - 7.75
  6 income brackets - Lowest $10,200; Highest $225,000.

Personal Exemption $ (single / joint) ....700 / 1,400
  Additional $1,000 if age 65 or over.

Standard Deduction $ (single / joint).........8,960 / 16,140
  Amounts are the maximum, reduced as income rises.

Reaches zero for single filers at $87,500 and for joint filers at $99,736.

Federal Income Tax Paid - Deduction Allowed	None
Social Security Income - Tax Exempt	Yes
Retired Military Pay - Tax Exempt	Yes
State & Local Government Pensions - Tax Exempt	Limits
Federal Civil Service Pensions - Tax Exempt	Limits
Railroad Retirement - Tax Exempt	Yes
Private Pension - Tax Exempt	Limits

Note: Limits include a maximum combined exemption of $5,000, with income limitations, for benefits from qualified plans.

VEHICLES

Registration Fees .... 1 Year
Automobile, $75.

Truck:
4,500 - 8,000 lbs, $75 - $106.
8,001 - 12,000 lbs, $155 - 209.

Camping trailer, $15.

Motor home fee varies by weight:
up to 12,000 lbs, $48.50 - $67.50
12,000 - 26,000 lbs, $80.50 - $106.50.
Over 26,000 lbs, $119.50.

Plus a $10 - $20 Wheel tax for the cities of Beloit, Mayville, Milwaukee, and St. Croix County.

Annual Vehicle Tax .... No
No property tax on vehicles.

State Emissions Test Required ....Yes
Every two years for vehicles under 8,501 lbs in these southern counties: Kenosha, Milwaukee, Ozaukee, Racine, Sheboygan, Washington, and Waukesha. Diesel powered vehicles are exempt. Web Site: www.dot.wisconsin.gov/drivers/vehicles/im.htm.

Vehicle Safety Inspection Required .... No
Mandatory Minimum Liability Insurance 50/100/55
Uninsured and Underinsured Motorists coverage is also required.

COST OF LIVING INDICATORS

Rank: 1 highest; 51 lowest

Cost of Living - average statewide (rank)	33
Per Capita Income (rank / $)	28 / 37,314

Median Household Income (rank / $)	22 / 52,103
Median House Value (rank / $)	27 / 168,500
Median Property Tax on Homes (rank)	09
Fuel - avg per gal $, Mar 2010 (diesel / gas)	2.89 / 2.69
Fuel Taxes - per gallon $ (diesel / gas)	0.573 / 0.513
Cigarette Tax - pack of 20 ($)	3.53
Tax Burden - average all taxes (rank)	10

STATE & LOCAL REVENUE SOURCES

Rank: 1 highest; 51 lowest
Rank and % of total revenue from:

Tax Revenue (see "Details" listed below)	24 / 41.80
Charges & Misc. Revenue	43 / 17.04
Federal Government	44 / 12.84
Utility Revenue	32 / 02.47
Insurance Trust Revenue	04 / 25.85

Tax Revenue Details (rank / %)

Property Tax	12 / 36.02
Sales & Gross Receipts	39 / 27.40
Individual Income Tax	15 / 27.14
Corporate Income Tax	26 / 03.96
Motor Vehicle License	27 / 01.57
Other Taxes	38 / 03.91

POPULATION

Rank: 1 highest; 51 lowest

State Population (rank / count)	20 / 5,654,774
Population Per Square Mile (rank / count)	29 / 86

VOTING

Registration Requirements: In-person registration deadline is the day of election.

Address Requirements: Physical/street address required.

Register by Mail: Yes, registration deadline is 21 days before election.

Absentee Voting: Yes, no excuse is required.

Web Site: http://elections.state.wi.us/

RESOURCES

Wisconsin State Government
Phone: 608-266-2211
Web Site: www.wisconsin.gov

Wisconsin Department of Revenue
Phone: 608-266-2772
Web Site: www.revenue.wi.gov

Wisconsin Division of Motor Vehicles
Phone: 800-924-3570
Web Site: www.dot.wisconsin.gov/drivers

Wisconsin Office of Tourism
Phone: 800-432-8747
Web Site: www.travelwisconsin.com

Wyoming

WEATHER

	Casper			Cheyenne		
	🌡	💧	❄	🌡	💧	❄
Jan	33/12	0.5	10	38/15	0.4	5.9
Feb	38/16	0.6	10.4	41/18	0.4	5.6
Mar	45/22	0.9	14	44/21	1	11.7
Apr	56/30	1.4	12.7	55/30	1.4	8.1
May	67/39	2.2	3.7	64/40	2.5	2.6
Jun	78/48	1.4	0.2	75/48	2.2	0
Jul	87/54	1.2	0	83/54	2.1	0
Aug	86/53	0.6	0	81/53	1.6	0
Sep	74/43	0.9	1.1	72/44	1.2	0.7
Oct	61/33	1	5.2	60/34	0.7	3.9
Nov	44/22	0.8	10.7	47/23	0.6	6.6
Dec	35/15	0.6	10.8	40/17	0.4	6
🌡	Average monthly high and low temperatures in degrees Fahrenheit.					
💧	Average monthly precipitation totals in inches.					
❄	Average monthly snowfall totals in inches.					

STATE AND LOCAL TAXES

State Sales Tax (%) 4.00
 Exempt: food and prescription drugs.

Local Sales Taxes (up to an additional %) 2.00

Inheritance Tax .... No

Estate Tax ....Yes
 Limited to federal estate tax collection.

PERSONAL INCOME TAXES

State Income Tax (%) .... None

Personal Exemption $ (single / joint) .... n/a

Standard Deduction $ (single / joint)............................... n/a

Federal Income Tax Paid - Deduction Allowed .... n/a

Social Security Income - Tax Exempt................................ n/a

Retired Military Pay - Tax Exempt .... n/a

State & Local Government Pensions - Tax Exempt .... n/a
Federal Civil Service Pensions - Tax Exempt .... n/a
Railroad Retirement - Tax Exempt .... n/a
Private Pension - Tax Exempt .... n/a

VEHICLES

Registration Fees .... 1 Year
   Rates available from the local county treasurers' office.
   Fees vary by vehicle type, age, and value. The Wyoming
   County Treasurer's Association provides a fee calculator
   at: www.wcta.us

Annual Vehicle Tax .... No
   All fees are included in the registration process.

State Emissions Test Required .... No
Vehicle Safety Inspection Required .... No
Mandatory Minimum Liability Insurance 25/50/20

COST OF LIVING INDICATORS

   Rank: 1 highest; 51 lowest

Cost of Living - average statewide (rank) 24
Per Capita Income (rank / $) .... 05 / 49,719
Median Household Income (rank / $) .... 19 / 54,735
Median House Value (rank / $).......................... 26 / 169,100
Median Property Tax on Homes (rank) 41
Fuel - avg per gal $, Mar 2010 (diesel / gas) .....2.79 / 2.56
Fuel Taxes - per gallon $ (diesel / gas)........... 0.384 / 0.324
Cigarette Tax - pack of 20 ($) 1.61
Tax Burden - average all taxes (rank) 49

STATE & LOCAL REVENUE SOURCES

   Rank: 1 highest; 51 lowest
   Rank and % of total revenue from:

Tax Revenue (see "Details" listed below) .... 39 / 38.02
Charges & Misc. Revenue.. 09 / 24.22
Federal Government .... 06 / 21.99
Utility Revenue .... 41 / 01.75
Insurance Trust Revenue... 35 / 14.02

   Tax Revenue Details (rank / %)

Property Tax.. 09 / 36.87
Sales & Gross Receipts .... 28 / 33.02
Individual Income Tax.. 44 / 0
Corporate Income Tax.. 46 / 0
Motor Vehicle License.. 10 / 02.53
Other Taxes .... 03 / 27.58

POPULATION

   Rank: 1 highest; 51 lowest

State Population (rank / count) ....51 / 544,270
Population Per Square Mile (rank / count) .... 50 / 6

VOTING

Registration Requirements: In-person registration deadline is the day of election.

Address Requirements: Physical/street address required.

Register by Mail: Yes, registration deadline is 30 days before election.

Absentee Voting: Yes, no excuse is required.

Web Site: http://soswy.state.wy.us/Elections/Elections.aspx

RESOURCES

Wyoming State Government
Phone: 307-777-7011
Web Site: www.wyoming.gov

Wyoming Department of Revenue
Phone: 307-777-5287
Web Site: http://revenue.state.wy.us

Wyoming Motor Vehicle Services
Phone: 307-777-4825
Web Site: www.dot.state.wy.us

Wyoming Office of Tourism
Phone: 800-225-5996
Web Site: www.wyomingtourism.org

State Income Tax

Tax Rates	%
Alabama	2 - 5
Alaska	none
Arizona	2.59 - 4.54
Arkansas	1 - 7
California	1.25 - 10.55
Colorado	4.63
Connecticut	3 - 6.5
Delaware	2.2 - 6.95
District of Columbia	4 - 8.5
Florida	none
Georgia	1 - 6
Hawaii	1.4 - 11
Idaho	1.6 - 7.8
Illinois	3
Indiana	3.4
Iowa	0.36 - 8.98
Kansas	3.5 - 6.45
Kentucky	2 - 6
Louisiana	2 - 6
Maine	2 - 8.5
Maryland	2 - 6.25
Massachusetts	5.3
Michigan	4.35
Minnesota	5.35 - 7.85
Mississippi	3 - 5
Missouri	1.5 - 6
Montana	1 - 6.9
Nebraska	2.56 - 6.84
Nevada	none
New Hampshire	limited
New Jersey	1.4 - 8.9
New Mexico	1.7 - 5.3
New York	4 - 8.97
North Carolina	6 - 7.75
North Dakota	1.84 - 4.86
Ohio	.587 - 5.925
Oklahoma	0.5 - 5.5
Oregon	5 - 11
Pennsylvania	3.07
Rhode Island	3.75 - 9.9
South Carolina	3 - 7
South Dakota	none
Tennessee	limited
Texas	none
Utah	5
Vermont	3.55 - 8.95
Virginia	2 - 5.75
Washington	none
West Virginia	3 - 6.5
Wisconsin	4.6 - 7.75
Wyoming	none

State and Local Sales Tax

Tax Rates (%)	State	Local
Alabama	4	8
Alaska	none	7
Arizona	6.3	1.125
Arkansas	6	6.5
California	8.25	2.5
Colorado	2.9	7
Connecticut	6	none
Delaware	none	none
District of Columbia	6	none
Florida	6	3.5
Georgia	4	3
Hawaii	4	0.5
Idaho	6	3
Illinois	6.25	5.25
Indiana	7	none
Iowa	6	1
Kansas	5.3	3
Kentucky	6	none
Louisiana	4	6.75
Maine	5	none
Maryland	6	none
Massachusetts	6.25	none
Michigan	6	none
Minnesota	6.875	2.5
Mississippi	7	4.5
Missouri	4.225	5.375
Montana	none	none
Nebraska	5.5	1.5
Nevada	6.85	0.875
New Hampshire	none	none
New Jersey	7	limited
New Mexico	5.375	2.68
New York	4	5
North Carolina	5.75	2.5
North Dakota	5	2.5
Ohio	5.5	2
Oklahoma	4.5	7
Oregon	none	none
Pennsylvania	6	2
Rhode Island	7	none
South Carolina	6	2
South Dakota	4	2.75
Tennessee	7	2.75
Texas	6.25	2
Utah	5.95	2.4
Vermont	6	1
Virginia	5	none
Washington	6.5	2.4
West Virginia	6	none
Wisconsin	5	0.6
Wyoming	4	2

Fuel Price & Tax

Diesel $ - **DP** / Tax - **DT**
Gas $ - **GP** / Tax - **GT**

	DP	GP	DT	GT
Alabama	2.79	2.63	0.444	0.374
Alaska	3.60	3.38	0.324	0.264
Arizona	2.90	2.67	0.434	0.374
Arkansas	2.77	2.59	0.472	0.402
California	3.09	3.01	0.438	0.378
Colorado	2.80	2.59	0.449	0.404
Connecticut	3.14	2.85	0.695	0.603
Delaware	2.92	2.66	0.464	0.414
District of Columbia	3.05	2.81	0.479	0.419
Florida	2.90	2.76	0.426	0.421
Georgia	2.81	2.65	0.422	0.330
Hawaii	3.93	3.46	0.415	0.355
Idaho	2.93	2.74	0.494	0.434
Illinois	2.96	2.76	0.459	0.374
Indiana	2.88	2.62	0.524	0.374
Iowa	2.81	2.65	0.479	0.404
Kansas	2.78	2.61	0.514	0.434
Kentucky	2.80	2.63	0.439	0.409
Louisiana	2.77	2.62	0.444	0.384
Maine	3.05	2.74	0.566	0.494
Maryland	2.91	2.68	0.487	0.419
Massachusetts	2.95	2.69	0.479	0.419
Michigan	2.85	2.64	0.403	0.383
Minnesota	2.90	2.69	0.516	0.456
Mississippi	2.76	2.61	0.428	0.368
Missouri	2.68	2.51	0.417	0.357
Montana	2.89	2.70	0.530	0.462
Nebraska	2.82	2.74	0.512	0.452
Nevada	2.88	2.79	0.522	0.422
New Hampshire	2.87	2.64	0.440	0.380
New Jersey	2.80	2.56	0.419	0.329
New Mexico	2.84	2.71	0.472	0.372
New York	3.12	2.87	0.478	0.436
North Carolina	2.85	2.68	0.546	0.486
North Dakota	2.98	2.78	0.474	0.414
Ohio	2.88	2.59	0.524	0.464
Oklahoma	2.67	2.55	0.384	0.354
Oregon	2.91	2.82	0.484	0.424
Pennsylvania	3.04	2.76	0.636	0.507
Rhode Island	2.98	2.75	0.574	0.514
South Carolina	2.74	2.56	0.412	0.352
South Dakota	2.89	2.72	0.484	0.424
Tennessee	2.77	2.60	0.428	0.398
Texas	2.76	2.57	0.444	0.384
Utah	2.90	2.74	0.489	0.429
Vermont	3.05	2.75	0.534	0.429
Virginia	2.81	2.61	0.425	0.365
Washington	3.06	2.91	0.619	0.559
West Virginia	2.94	2.74	0.565	0.505
Wisconsin	2.89	2.69	0.573	0.513
Wyoming	2.79	2.56	0.384	0.324

*Social Security-**S** / Military-**M** / State or Local-**L** / Federal Civil Service-**F** / Railroad Retirement-**R** / Private Pension-**P***						

State Deductions for Pension Income

Pension Type	S	M	L	F	R	P
Alabama	Yes	Yes	Yes	Yes	Yes	Limits
Alaska	Yes	Yes	Yes	Yes	Yes	Yes
Arizona	Yes	Limits	Limits	Limits	Yes	No
Arkansas	Yes	Limits	Limits	Limits	Yes	Limits
California	Yes	No	No	No	Yes	No
Colorado	Yes	Limits	Limits	Limits	Yes	Limits
Connecticut	Limits	Limits	No	No	Yes	No
Delaware	Yes	Limits	Limits	Limits	Yes	Limits
District of Columbia	Yes	Limits	Limits	Limits	Yes	No
Florida	Yes	Yes	Yes	Yes	Yes	Yes
Georgia	Yes	Limits	Limits	Limits	Yes	Limits
Hawaii	Yes	Yes	Yes	Yes	Yes	Yes
Idaho	Yes	Limits	Limits	Limits	Yes	No
Illinois	Yes	Yes	Yes	Yes	Yes	Limits
Indiana	Yes	Limits	No	Limits	Yes	No
Iowa	Limits	Limits	Limits	Limits	Yes	Limits
Kansas	Limits	Yes	Limits	Yes	Yes	No
Kentucky	Limits	Limits	Limits	Limits	Yes	Limits
Louisiana	Yes	Yes	Limits	Yes	Yes	Limits
Maine	Yes	Limits	Limits	Limits	Yes	Limits
Maryland	Yes	Limits	Limits	Limits	Yes	Limits
Massachusetts	Yes	Yes	Limits	Yes	Yes	No
Michigan	Yes	Yes	Limits	Yes	Yes	Limits
Minnesota	Limits	No	No	No	Yes	No
Mississippi	Yes	Yes	Yes	Yes	Yes	Limits
Missouri	Limits	Limits	Limits	Limits	Yes	Limits
Montana	Limits	Limits	Limits	Limits	Yes	Limits
Nebraska	Limits	No	No	No	Yes	No
Nevada	Yes	Yes	Yes	Yes	Yes	Yes
New Hampshire	Yes	Yes	Yes	Yes	Yes	Yes
New Jersey	Yes	Yes	Limits	Limits	Yes	Limits
New Mexico	Limits	Limits	Limits	Limits	Yes	Limits
New York	Yes	Yes	Limits	Yes	Yes	Limits
North Carolina	Yes	Limits	Limits	Limits	Yes	Limits
North Dakota	Limits	Limits	Limits	Limits	Yes	No
Ohio	Yes	Yes	No	No	Yes	No
Oklahoma	Yes	Limits	Limits	Limits	Yes	Limits
Oregon	Yes	Limits	Limits	Limits	Yes	Limits
Pennsylvania	Yes	Yes	Yes	Yes	Yes	Yes
Rhode Island	Limits	No	No	No	Yes	No
South Carolina	Yes	Limits	Limits	Limits	Yes	Limits
South Dakota	Yes	Yes	Yes	Yes	Yes	Yes
Tennessee	Yes	Yes	Yes	Yes	Yes	Yes
Texas	Yes	Yes	Yes	Yes	Yes	Yes
Utah	Limits	Limits	Limits	Limits	Limits	Limits
Vermont	Limits	No	No	No	Yes	No
Virginia	Yes	Limits	Limits	Limits	Yes	Limits
Washington	Yes	Yes	Yes	Yes	Yes	Yes
West Virginia	Limits	Limits	Limits	Limits	Yes	Limits
Wisconsin	Yes	Yes	Limits	Limits	Yes	Limits
Wyoming	Yes	Yes	Yes	Yes	Yes	Yes

*Vehicle Tax - **VT** Emissions Test - **ET** Safety Inspection - **SI***			

Vehicles

	VT	ET	SI
Alabama	Yes	No	No
Alaska	Yes	Yes	No
Arizona	Yes	Yes	No
Arkansas	Yes	No	No
California	Yes	Yes	No
Colorado	Yes	Yes	No
Connecticut	Yes	Yes	Yes
Delaware	No	Yes	Yes
District of Columbia	No	Yes	Yes
Florida	No	No	No
Georgia	Yes	Yes	No
Hawaii	Yes	No	Yes
Idaho	Yes	Yes	No
Illinois	No	Yes	No
Indiana	Yes	Yes	No
Iowa	Yes	No	No
Kansas	Yes	No	No
Kentucky	Yes	No	No
Louisiana	No	Yes	Yes
Maine	Yes	Yes	Yes
Maryland	No	Yes	Yes
Massachusetts	Yes	Yes	Yes
Michigan	Yes	No	No
Minnesota	Yes	No	No
Mississippi	Yes	No	Yes
Missouri	Yes	Yes	Yes
Montana	Yes	No	No
Nebraska	Yes	No	No
Nevada	Yes	Yes	No
New Hampshire	Yes	Yes	Yes
New Jersey	No	Yes	Yes
New Mexico	No	Yes	No
New York	No	Yes	Yes
North Carolina	Yes	Yes	Yes
North Dakota	No	No	No
Ohio	No	Yes	No
Oklahoma	No	No	No
Oregon	No	Yes	No
Pennsylvania	No	Yes	Yes
Rhode Island	Yes	Yes	Yes
South Carolina	Yes	No	No
South Dakota	No	No	No
Tennessee	No	Yes	No
Texas	No	Yes	Yes
Utah	Yes	Yes	Yes
Vermont	No	Yes	Yes
Virginia	Yes	Yes	Yes
Washington	No	Yes	No
West Virginia	Yes	No	Yes
Wisconsin	No	Yes	No
Wyoming	No	No	No

Tax Revenue - **TR** / Charges & Misc. - **CM** Federal Government - **FG** / Utility - **UR** Insurance Trust - **IT**	**State Revenue - Rank**				
	TR	**CM**	**FG**	**UR**	**IT**
Alabama	48	7	14	8	26
Alaska	49	1	26	37	34
Arizona	14	37	22	4	45
Arkansas	27	39	12	23	19
California	42	41	49	10	2
Colorado	30	12	48	15	14
Connecticut	1	51	46	37	29
Delaware	31	2	40	22	41
District of Columbia	12	50	3	7	51
Florida	22	17	43	13	21
Georgia	16	26	18	9	44
Hawaii	4	38	24	43	32
Idaho	35	13	28	40	9
Illinois	6	48	39	30	8
Indiana	19	6	23	18	47
Iowa	32	11	25	29	23
Kansas	5	29	38	12	38
Kentucky	28	31	13	21	27
Louisiana	41	35	2	31	39
Maine	13	44	10	47	25
Maryland	3	46	34	45	24
Massachusetts	11	42	33	20	22
Michigan	29	10	31	34	20
Minnesota	17	27	41	28	12
Mississippi	51	34	1	30	28
Missouri	36	30	20	24	7
Montana	43	24	7	46	10
Nebraska	34	25	37	1	48
Nevada	15	21	50	19	18
New Hampshire	10	8	27	48	43
New Jersey	2	47	45	41	31
New Mexico	44	23	8	35	15
New York	9	49	32	17	16
North Carolina	20	20	15	16	42
North Dakota	26	14	9	39	37
Ohio	40	40	35	38	3
Oklahoma	33	19	16	14	30
Oregon	50	22	42	27	1
Pennsylvania	18	32	30	36	13
Rhode Island	21	45	17	42	11
South Carolina	46	3	19	5	40
South Dakota	47	33	11	25	5
Tennessee	45	18	21	2	46
Texas	23	16	29	11	33
Utah	37	5	36	6	36
Vermont	7	36	5	26	49
Virginia	8	15	51	33	17
Washington	38	28	47	3	6
West Virginia	25	4	4	44	50
Wisconsin	24	43	44	32	4
Wyoming	39	9	6	41	35

Tax Revenue-**TR** / Charges & Misc.-**CM** Federal Government-**FG** / Utility-**UR** Insurance Trust-**IT**	**State Revenue - %**				
	TR	**CM**	**FG**	**UR**	**IT**
Alabama	33.08	25.18	19.23	6.37	16.13
Alaska	32.00	35.51	16.47	1.95	14.07
Arizona	45.41	18.04	16.96	7.75	11.84
Arkansas	40.72	17.77	19.99	3.52	18.01
California	36.99	17.48	11.84	5.51	28.19
Colorado	39.83	23.63	12.22	4.67	19.64
Connecticut	56.88	12.85	12.34	1.95	15.99
Delaware	39.65	29.38	13.70	4.15	13.13
District of Columbia	45.59	13.66	26.33	7.14	7.28
Florida	42.21	21.85	13.29	4.87	17.78
Georgia	43.60	20.25	18.14	5.67	12.34
Hawaii	48.44	17.98	16.50	1.56	15.52
Idaho	38.58	22.72	16.02	1.77	20.91
Illinois	46.10	16.05	14.15	2.73	20.97
Indiana	43.03	25.40	16.69	4.32	10.56
Iowa	39.51	23.68	16.49	3.12	17.20
Kansas	47.99	19.68	14.17	4.93	13.24
Kentucky	40.53	19.31	19.89	4.16	16.11
Louisiana	37.58	18.21	28.41	2.60	13.21
Maine	45.51	16.95	20.40	0.92	16.22
Maryland	50.17	16.38	14.99	1.29	17.18
Massachusetts	45.70	17.26	15.16	4.23	17.65
Michigan	40.05	24.08	15.54	2.38	17.96
Minnesota	43.54	19.72	13.49	3.21	20.03
Mississippi	29.50	18.60	33.06	2.73	16.10
Missouri	38.56	19.52	17.38	3.42	21.12
Montana	35.62	20.85	21.96	1.18	20.40
Nebraska	38.63	20.26	14.66	15.92	10.52
Nevada	45.00	21.22	10.65	4.28	18.85
New Hampshire	45.75	24.71	16.25	0.87	12.42
New Jersey	53.98	16.17	12.36	1.75	15.74
New Mexico	35.55	21.13	21.36	2.37	19.59
New York	45.77	14.84	15.43	4.42	19.54
North Carolina	42.72	21.24	18.79	4.63	12.62
North Dakota	41.02	22.55	20.98	1.82	13.63
Ohio	37.78	17.63	14.93	1.92	27.74
Oklahoma	39.36	21.39	18.72	4.68	15.85
Oregon	30.54	21.17	13.43	3.24	31.63
Pennsylvania	43.07	19.31	15.62	2.21	19.80
Rhode Island	42.57	16.93	18.70	1.72	20.08
South Carolina	34.98	26.49	17.89	7.49	13.16
South Dakota	33.84	19.07	20.00	3.28	23.82
Tennessee	35.21	21.43	17.10	14.81	11.45
Texas	41.86	21.88	15.84	5.42	15.00
Utah	38.40	25.53	14.91	7.33	13.83
Vermont	46.06	18.10	22.56	3.26	10.02
Virginia	45.92	22.12	10.61	2.44	18.91
Washington	38.07	19.70	12.32	8.02	21.89
West Virginia	41.19	25.85	23.07	1.38	8.52
Wisconsin	41.80	17.04	12.84	2.47	25.85
Wyoming	38.02	24.22	21.99	1.75	14.02

Property Tax - **PT** / Sales & Gross Rec. - **SG** / Individual Inc. Tax - **II** / Corp. Inc. Tax - **CI** / Motor Vehicle - **MV** / Other Taxes - **OT** **Tax Revenue - Rank**	PT	SG	II	CI	MV	OT
Alabama	47	11	31	29	23	18
Alaska	42	50	44	1	31	1
Arizona	33	9	38	25	37	40
Arkansas	50	5	26	27	30	47
California	37	33	7	9	28	25
Colorado	22	23	18	42	32	34
Connecticut	7	44	9	28	38	45
Delaware	48	49	13	5	39	2
District of Columbia	24	41	20	7	44	9
Florida	10	8	44	32	24	14
Georgia	27	15	17	35	41	51
Hawaii	45	7	25	45	5	50
Idaho	39	21	11	27	6	32
Illinois	8	27	37	14	11	36
Indiana	25	19	22	20	35	46
Iowa	17	32	21	37	3	43
Kansas	21	22	23	21	26	39
Kentucky	43	20	12	6	22	30
Louisiana	49	6	36	24	43	17
Maine	11	35	24	33	27	35
Maryland	36	45	2	38	23	19
Massachusetts	13	46	3	8	40	42
Michigan	6	30	35	18	13	48
Minnesota	34	31	8	16	15	33
Mississippi	35	10	39	25	30	28
Missouri	30	18	16	44	33	31
Montana	15	47	19	13	2	6
Nebraska	16	29	29	36	19	23
Nevada	29	2	44	46	24	8
New Hampshire	1	48	42	2	20	22
New Jersey	3	43	30	12	41	29
New Mexico	51	12	40	10	7	5
New York	28	42	5	3	42	26
North Carolina	41	26	4	17	18	37
North Dakota	31	25	41	15	14	4
Ohio	26	34	10	41	17	27
Oklahoma	46	16	28	19	1	7
Oregon	19	51	1	31	4	16
Pennsylvania	23	37	19	23	27	11
Rhode Island	5	38	32	30	36	49
South Carolina	18	24	27	43	34	21
South Dakota	14	4	44	34	12	24
Tennessee	38	3	43	11	9	15
Texas	4	13	44	46	16	12
Utah	40	14	14	22	35	41
Vermont	2	36	34	39	8	44
Virginia	20	40	6	40	25	20
Washington	32	1	44	46	21	13
West Virginia	44	17	33	4	29	10
Wisconsin	12	39	15	26	27	38
Wyoming	9	28	44	46	10	3

Property Tax-**PT** / Sales & Gross Rec.-**SG** / Individual Inc. Tax-**II** / Corp. Inc. Tax-**CI** / Motor Vehicle-**MV** / Other Taxes-**OT** **Tax Revenue - %**	PT	SG	II	CI	MV	OT
Alabama	15.57	47.73	22.70	3.76	1.70	8.54
Alaska	20.95	9.85	0	16.44	1.41	51.35
Arizona	26.66	48.42	16.06	4.23	1.02	3.61
Arkansas	14.69	53.23	23.62	3.95	1.43	3.08
California	24.13	31.35	30.83	6.45	1.53	5.71
Colorado	30.38	35.39	25.74	2.57	1.39	4.53
Connecticut	38.26	23.54	30.03	3.91	0.96	3.30
Delaware	15.55	12.78	29.33	8.26	0.95	33.13
District of Columbia	29.20	25.62	25.29	8.03	0.50	11.36
Florida	36.78	48.91	0	3.35	1.63	9.33
Georgia	28.71	38.53	26.54	3.07	0.87	2.28
Hawaii	17.32	51.79	23.76	1.54	3.30	2.29
Idaho	23.40	35.73	29.53	3.95	2.75	4.64
Illinois	37.15	33.76	17.08	5.33	2.50	4.18
Indiana	29.12	37.17	24.72	4.68	1.19	3.12
Iowa	33.07	31.65	25.07	2.97	3.83	3.41
Kansas	30.46	35.42	24.19	4.65	1.58	3.70
Kentucky	18.83	37.09	29.49	8.10	1.76	4.73
Louisiana	14.84	53.09	18.27	4.28	0.64	8.88
Maine	36.58	30.07	24.13	3.27	1.57	4.38
Maryland	24.19	23.40	39.70	2.89	1.70	8.12
Massachusetts	34.38	19.21	35.49	6.56	0.94	3.42
Michigan	39.19	32.03	18.63	4.82	2.45	2.88
Minnesota	25.86	31.81	30.56	5.00	2.18	4.59
Mississippi	25.27	47.90	16.05	4.23	1.43	5.12
Missouri	27.40	37.59	26.93	2.04	1.38	4.66
Montana	33.83	16.36	25.46	5.46	4.77	14.12
Nebraska	33.44	32.38	23.12	2.98	1.82	6.26
Nevada	27.53	58.19	0	0	1.63	12.65
New Hampshire	61.39	15.50	2.27	12.56	1.81	6.47
New Jersey	41.77	23.89	22.80	5.61	0.87	5.06
New Mexico	13.54	46.93	15.80	6.17	2.73	14.83
New York	28.41	24.26	31.83	9.26	0.70	5.54
North Carolina	22.54	34.01	32.66	4.83	2.00	3.96
North Dakota	26.81	35.12	12.16	5.24	2.22	18.45
Ohio	28.99	31.24	29.85	2.63	2.12	5.17
Oklahoma	16.16	38.11	23.22	4.70	5.12	12.69
Oregon	31.05	8.67	44.02	3.63	3.61	9.02
Pennsylvania	29.59	28.63	25.46	4.38	1.57	10.37
Rhode Island	41.02	28.62	22.68	3.74	1.10	2.84
South Carolina	31.11	35.24	23.47	2.26	1.35	6.57
South Dakota	34.30	54.08	0	3.21	2.46	5.95
Tennessee	23.83	57.07	1.38	6.10	2.54	9.08
Texas	41.68	46.73	0	0	2.13	9.46
Utah	22.89	39.12	28.75	4.48	1.19	3.57
Vermont	42.19	29.21	19.83	2.84	2.59	3.34
Virginia	30.94	26.37	31.63	2.72	1.59	6.75
Washington	26.78	62.05	0	0	1.78	9.39
West Virginia	18.62	37.89	22.29	8.83	1.45	10.92
Wisconsin	36.02	27.40	27.14	3.96	1.57	3.91
Wyoming	36.87	33.02	0	0	2.53	27.58

Cost of Living - **CL** / Per Capita Income - **PC**
Household Income - **HI** / House Value - **HV**
Property Tax - **PT** / Tax Burden - **TB**

Cost of Living Indicators

	CL	PC	HI	HV	PT	TB
Alabama	41	42	47	45	50	39
Alaska	4	8	4	18	13	51
Arizona	16	43	23	17	34	42
Arkansas	49	48	49	49	47	15
California	3	12	9	2	10	6
Colorado	17	14	14	16	31	35
Connecticut	8	2	3	8	2	3
Delaware	21	17	11	15	40	25
District of Columbia	2	1	10	3	19	8
Florida	22	22	34	19	22	48
Georgia	45	41	24	29	35	17
Hawaii	1	18	5	1	32	5
Idaho	39	44	35	25	37	14
Illinois	32	13	17	22	7	31
Indiana	40	40	33	39	38	29
Iowa	36	30	30	44	29	32
Kansas	42	25	26	42	27	22
Kentucky	46	47	48	46	44	26
Louisiana	30	31	44	38	51	43
Maine	13	34	38	24	21	16
Maryland	6	6	1	6	11	4
Massachusetts	11	4	6	5	6	24
Michigan	28	35	31	32	17	28
Minnesota	20	11	13	21	20	13
Mississippi	38	51	50	50	48	37
Missouri	44	36	36	35	36	33
Montana	19	39	42	28	30	41
Nebraska	48	26	29	40	18	18
Nevada	15	19	16	9	25	50
New Hampshire	12	10	7	12	3	47
New Jersey	5	3	2	4	1	1
New Mexico	25	45	43	31	43	40
New York	7	7	18	7	4	2
North Carolina	31	37	37	33	39	21
North Dakota	34	21	40	47	26	34
Ohio	37	33	32	34	24	7
Oklahoma	51	29	46	48	45	20
Oregon	14	32	27	14	16	27
Pennsylvania	23	20	25	30	15	12
Rhode Island	9	16	20	11	5	11
South Carolina	27	47	41	36	46	38
South Dakota	43	27	39	43	28	46
Tennessee	50	38	45	37	42	45
Texas	47	24	28	41	14	44
Utah	29	50	15	20	33	23
Vermont	10	23	21	23	8	9
Virginia	26	9	8	13	23	19
Washington	18	15	12	10	12	36
West Virginia	35	49	51	51	49	30
Wisconsin	33	28	22	27	9	10
Wyoming	24	5	19	26	41	49